Liddle

Gilbert Van Deusen Liddle (7) and Rebecca (Bradley Watson) Liddle of the
John Liddle branch and their homestead at Colon, Mich.

Martha (Liddle) Gifford (35), Vineland, New Jersey
Author of this volume

Hermitage Castle was built in 1244 by Lord Nicholas de Soules and stands on the northern bank of the Liddle River, which flows between Scotland and England, emptying into the Irish Sea

GENEALOGY

of the

LIDDLE FAMILY

MARTHA (LIDDLE) GIFFORD

Vineland, N. J.

Author

Designed and Arranged by
RAYMOND M. SIDES (88)

Notice

In many older books, foxing (or discoloration) occurs and, in
some instances, print lightens with wear and age. Reprinted
books, such as this, often duplicate these flaws, notwith-
standing efforts to reduce or eliminate them. The pages of
this reprint have been digitally enhanced and, where possible,
the flaws eliminated in order to provide clarity of content and
a pleasant reading experience.

Genealogy of the Liddle Family

Originally published
n.p.
circa 1922

Reprinted by:

Janaway Publishing, Inc.
732 Kelsey Ct.
Santa Maria, California 93454
(805) 925-1038
www.janawaygenealogy.com

2012

ISBN 13: 978-1-59641-265-1

Contents

Page

Frontispiece . . . .

Historical Sketch of Liddesdale   3

Chart of Descendants   8

John Liddle Branch 10

Van Deusen Family Records 31

Trubey Family Records 34

Von Crapser Family Records 34

Van Antwerpen Family Records 35

Watson Family Records 36

Illustration 37

Robert Liddle Branch 37

Adam Liddle Branch 59

Index 67

Historical Sketch of Liddesdale

LIDDESDALE SCOTLAND is the much contested district of the border and forms the wedge-like termination of Roxburghshire, running a little into Dumfrieshire. Thomas Wake claiming Liddesdale caused a long border warfare in 1566.

Liddesdale belonged to the crown and the most notable of its fortresses or Peel Towers is the Castle Hermitage, where Queen Mary visited Bothwell in 1566. Hermitage Castle is said to have been built by Lord Nicholas de Sules about the year 1244, who then owned all of Liddesdale.

This castle is the best existing example of a border fortress in Scotland. Its remote position in the midst of a stretch of desolate country and on the edge of a deep morass bears out the grim character of the tales associated with it.

The Sules family forfeited their estate in 1320 and Hermitage went to the Grahams' and then by the marriage of Mary Graham, to the Knight of Liddesdale, William Douglass.

In 1492 Patric Hepburn, first Earl of Bothwell, exchanged Bothwell Castle on the Clyde, for Hermitage and Liddesdale. On the forfeiture of Francis Stewart, the last Earl of Bothwell, Hermitage went by grant to the Earl of Buccleuch, and is still owned by his descendants.

Not far from Liddesdale, was fought the battle of Flodden Field where on September 9, 1513, so many Scotsmen perished.

The ancient name of the river was Lid. The modern name of Liddle or Liddal includes both the name of the stream and the dale or del through which it flows. The addition of dale to Liddel, is a pleonasm, del and dale meaning the same. However, the name Liddle, Lyddel as applied to the river appears to have been established by the year 1250 or possibly earlier, though the ancient name sometimes appears much later. As an illustration, Jeffrey quotes Drummond of Hawthornden as singing of "The Lid with curled streams."

The manner of spelling the valley's name varied so much in different localities and epochs of history that the derivatives are bewildering. The spellings most frequently found are, Liddisdaill, Lyddesdale, Liddersdail, Liddisdale, etc., Liddesdale being the present established form.

Documents have not been found recording the direct line of lineage from the family of Lord Sules to the Liddle ancestry, but in A. Jeffrey's *History of Roxburghshire*, Vol. IV, is recorded a Randolph de Sules of the family of Lydal, who was made Provost of Roxburgh in 1296. That family of Sules Lords, as they were named Sules, built Hermitage Castle and were later Lords of Liddesdale. These Sules Lords are buried in a small enclosure beside Hermitage Castle.

It is hardly disputable that the Liddles are other than a branch of this Lydal family of Randolph de Sules, because both the names Liddle and Liddesdale have undergone many different forms of spelling since the thirteenth century. In official records and historical documents there are numerous instances where the same parcel of land or family name is referred to with a variation in spelling. In Vol. IV, *History of Roxburghshire*, Jeffrey also records a Richard de Sules whose family name was Lydal marrying in 1279 a Muriel Lobdel of Robertson. This town is about two miles from New Castleton, and it was here that John and Robert Liddle, first recorded in this book, were born.

Lord William Sules's reputation for brutality was even in that rough age such that he was commonly looked upon as inhuman. The people on his Liddesdale estate were constantly petitioning for relief from his acts of barbarism until one day, tired out with the never-ending complaints, King Alexander III exclaimed, "Oh boil him if you wish but let me hear no more of him!" It was a literal age, the King was taken at his word and the suggestion thus given was cheerfully followed. Lord Sules wrapped in a sheet of lead was carried by his own people to a spot called the "Ninestane Rig" about a mile from the Castle, Hermitage, and boiled in a huge caldron which was afterward preserved at Skelf Hill on a spot now marked by a circle of stones.

Extracts
from "The History of Selkirkshire or Chronicles of Ettrick Forest"

T. Craig Brown, Vol. I. Printed by Thomas and Archibald
Constoble of Edinburgh, 1886, for David Douglas.
Chapter v. 1329 to 1488.

*Page 79 quotes from King James' accounts of Ettrick Forest
for 1456, as follows:*

"Remission of rent for one steading was granted to Thomas
Cranstoune of that ilk, as bailie of the forest; Sir Walter Scot, as
master ranger of Ettrick; William Middelmest, as master
ranger of Yarrow; Robert Lidale, as ranger of Yarrow; George
Pringil, as master ranger of Tweed, and David Pringil, as ranger
of Tweed."

quoted from
"Other Items of Discharge"

"To Mr. Richard Forbes, when comptroller, per Robert
Liddale, ranger of Yarrow, toward the expense of the king's
household and the wages of his various servants."

quoted from page 106, as follows:

"In 1476 The Sheriff of Selkirk was ordered to see that one
Quintin Hog fulfilled an appointment; and next year Master
George Liddale—probably a relative of the ranger of Yarrow—
appears in a charter as Rector of the Forest," etc.

*Quoted from records of Court of Justiciary at
Selkirk before Lord Gray, etc. 17th, 18th, 19th, November, 1502
Saturday, 19th.*

"Remission of James Davidson in Quhitmerhall for art and
part of theft of a horse, a bonnet (pelei) a tepe and a sword
from Robert Liddale at the time of his slaughter. Ralf Ker of
Prymsydloch—surety, the said James Davidson should underly
the law at the next 'aire' of Selkirk, for art and part of the
cruel slaughter of Robert Liddale," etc.

IN 1727, Sir John Liddle owned an estate near that of Sir William Johnstone's, Westerhall, Langholm, Scotland, and it is likely that this estate is the tract associated with the tale handed down of a grant having been lost to the family of Liddles, resultant from numerous border insurrections at that time.

It is related that the title to an old Scottish estate was in dispute and that the contending Liddle heirs had collected the necessary records and proofs of inheritance to establish their claim indisputably.

The courier with the documents was traveling on horseback through a wild and rugged section to the country to present the credentials to the proper authorities when he was murdered, the documents stolen and his body thrown into a well where it was later discovered. All evidence indicated that the deed had been committed by an employee of the rival claimant, who was later adjudged the entitled heir by the courts.

It seems probable that Sir John Liddle who owned the above estate in 1727 was the father of Robert and John Liddle, our first American ancestors, because their birth dates of 1741 and 1748 respectively correspond with the period when Sir John would be rearing his family. This is further substantiated by the fact that they lived on the same grant of land and bore the same Christian name. There was trouble in Scotland over property at the time Robert and John came to America and according to facts or tales, handed down to the present genereration, from father to son, it was the cause of their emigration.

* * *

References

Encyclopedia Britannica, XVI, 588

Alexander Jeffrey, *History and Antiquitus of Roxburghshire.*
Edinburgh: Seton & Mackenzie, 1864.

Lord Sules

On a circle of stones they placed the pot,
A circle of stones but barely nine;
And heated it red and fiery hot,
Till burnished brass and glimmering sheen.
They rolled him up in a sheet of lead,
A sheet of lead for a funeral pall,
And plunged him into the caldron red,
And melted him, lead and bones and all.
On Skelf Hill the caldron still
The men of Liddesdale can show.
On the spot they placed the pot
The grass nor harebell ne'er will grow.

Extract from
Bothwell's Lament
(Part Second)

For I was reared amidst the hills,
Within a border home.
When rushing from their rocky glenns
The mountain torrents come.
Oh, Hermitage, by Liddel's side,
My old ancestral tower,
Oh, were I now but Lord of thee
Not owning half my power.
For in the days of reckless pride
I held, but cast away,
I would not leave the border keep
Until my dying day.
Who owns thee now fair Hermitage?
Who sits within thy wall?
What banners flutter in the breeze
Above that stately hall?
Does yet the court-yard ring with tramp
Of horses and of men;
Do bay of hounds and bugle-note
Sound merry from the glen?
Or art thou as thy master is,
A rent and ruined pile,
What matters it? These eyes of mine
Shall never see thee more;
Still in my thoughts thou must abide
As stately as of yore.

I

Last Scottish Generation

John Liddle 1

1st Am. Gen. John Br.

| 1a | John Liddle Jr. 2 | 2a | Adam Liddle 3 | 3a | 3b | 3c | 4 | 4a | 4b |

2nd Am. Gen. John Br.

John 5 Liddle	6	Gilbert 7 Liddle	Moses 8 Liddle	Eliza 9 Madaw	Nancy 10 McKinley	Mathew 11 Liddle	Cathern 12 Young	Getty 13 Rhode	14	15
16—27		30—38	39—41	42	43—47	48	49—53	54		
Jane		Henry	Sarah	Wallace	Gilbert	John	James	Jennie		
Alvina		Charles	Morris		Caroline		Emeline			
Fannie		Harriet	Noyes		Hays		Jacob			
Hirum		Gilbert			Mariette		Martha			
Philo		Julia			Byron		Gilbert			
Elizabeth		Martha								
Caroline		Marie								
John		Katherine								
Cathern		Henry								
Byron										
Harriet										
William										
Twins										

2nd Am. Gen. Adam Br.

Jacob 5 Liddle	Tryphosa 6 Handy	Adaline 7 Partridge	Adam 8 Liddle	9	Anna 10 Richtmyer	11
12—17	18—19	20—21	22—23		24—27	
Charles	Minerva	Allie	Perry		Estella	
Frank	Harvey	Rosella	John		Rodella	
Mary					Sarah	
Helen					Eva	
Ella						
William						

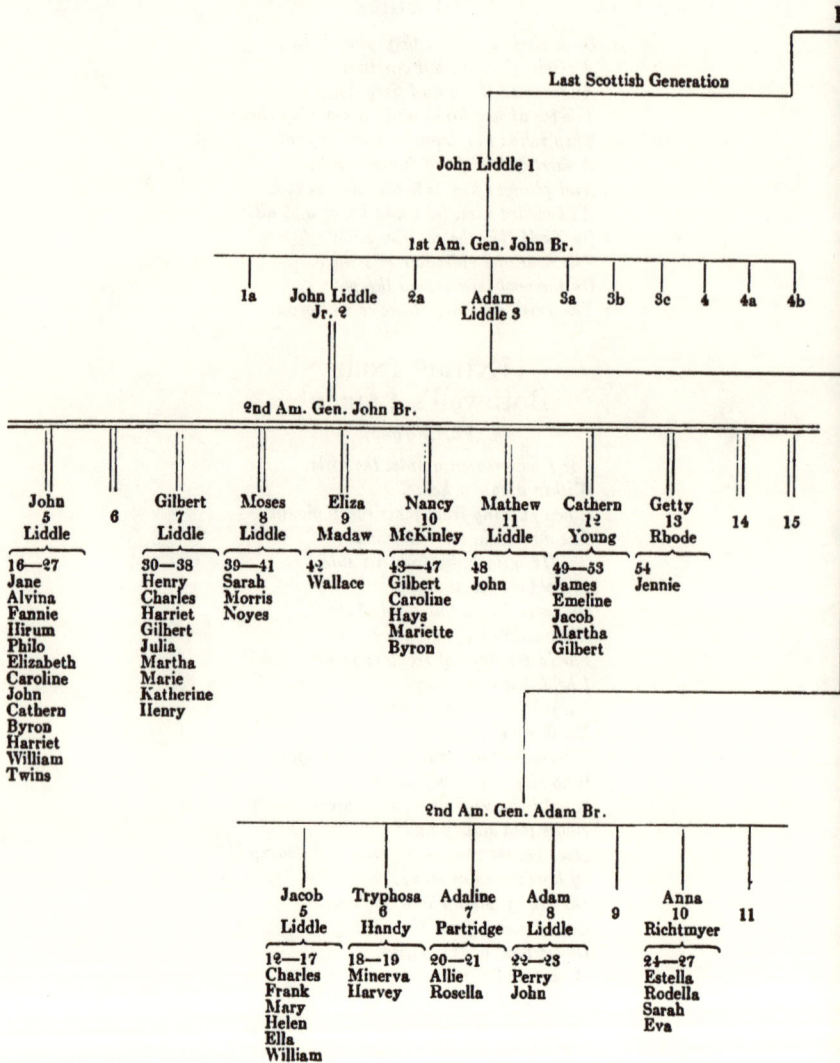

Indicates Van Deusen and Van Antwerp lineage

8

Last Scottish Generation

Robert Liddle 1

1st Am. Gen. Robert Br.

| Thomas Liddle 2 | 3 | 4 | 5 | Alexander Liddle 6 | 7 | John Liddle 8 |

2nd Gen. Am. Robert Br. 2nd Gen. Robert Br.

| Robert 16 Liddle | 17 | Alexander 18 Liddle | Anna 19 McMillan | John 20 Liddle | William 21 Liddle | James 22 Liddle | Mary 23 Jones | 24 | Robert 25 Liddle | William 26 Liddle |

42—52b		53—62	63—68	69—75	76—77	77a-b	78—83		84—87	88—96
Alexander		Alexander	Andrew	Alexander	William	Mary	Delos		John	Francis
Abigail		William	John	Mary	Warren	Abram	Mary		Sarah	William
Mary		Lea	James	George			Beatta		Nancy	Margaret
Ann		Margaret	Robert	William			Mary		Robert	John
Charles		John	Benjamin	Elizabeth			Nancy			Albertus
Thomas		Mary	Mary	Ida			Alexander			James
Abram		Elizabeth		Mary						Mary
Robert		Thomas								Robert
Angus		Sarah								Janet
Duncan										
Jeanette										
John										
Sarah										

2nd Gen. Robert Br.

| Alexander 9 Liddle | 10 | 11 | 12 | Romeyn 13 Liddle | Jane 14 Wright | 15 |

27—34				35	36—41	
Thomas				James	John	
Stewart					Jane	
Mary					Henry	
Sarah					Thomas	
Jeanette					Robert	
John					Edward	
Robert						
Ida						

9

First Generation
John Liddle Branch

1   JOHN LIDDLE, born in Roxburghshire, Scotland, November 28, 1748, came to America in 1775 with his brother Robert Liddle and family, consisting of his wife and four children, one, Betty being born on the voyage. John was not married when he left Scotland.

These brothers came from New Castleton, Liddesdale district of Roxburghshire, Scotland, situated on the Liddel River and near Sir William Johnstone's Estate "Westerhall," Langholm.

John settled in Fonda, Montgomery County, New York, while Robert settled at Princeton, Schenectady County, New York. (See Robert Liddle records.) John Liddle was married at Fonda, Montgomery County, New York, by the Pastor of the Reformed Church Reverend Thomas Romeyn, to Elizabeth Everson of Fonda, New York, May 2, 1776. She died at the age of 67. No record of her birth and no record of John Liddle's death, nor where they are buried has been found but it is believed they were buried in a private cemetery on the farm now owned by Arthur Van Epps at Fultonville, New York, which has been neglected. Some of the headstones have been plowed under, while others were thrown along the stone fence and badly broken. The author has placed a headstone in his memory at Colon, Michigan, where two of his grandsons are buried: Gilbert (7) and John Liddle (5).

He was a Revolutionary soldier and served as drummer and fifer in Captain Robert McKeen's Company of Colonel Cornelius D. Wyncoop's Regiment. His name is spelled "Liddel." (Reference: Quartermaster-General's records at Washington, D. C.) He also served as fifer in Captain Abraham Veeder's Company of Colonel Frederick Fisher's Regiment of Tryon County, New York, Militia, Mohawk district. (Reference: New York State Library.) In this company his name is spelled

"Lidel." These records were damaged in the fire of 1911, when the Library was burned.

The records of John Liddle and Elizabeth Everson, the baptism of their children, the marriage of John Liddle, Jr. and Elizabeth Van Deusen, and the baptism of their children, were kindly furnished by Mrs. William Van Deusen of Fonda, New York, who copied them from the Reformed Church records.

The data of the Adam Liddle records was not received until the arrangement of the John Liddle, Jr. (2) genealogy was compiled. Therefore the record of the Adam genealogy is compiled separately. Adam and John Jr. were brothers.

Children of John Liddle and Elizabeth Everson Liddle all born in Fonda, Montgomery County, New York:

1A JANNETTE LIDDLE, born November 28, 1778.
2 JOHN LIDDLE, JR., born October 15, 1780. Baptized November 12, 1780, by Reverend Thomas Romeyn. Witnesses: John Vrooman and Engeltye (Adaline) Collier. The family Bible records his birth October 18, 1780, but does not mention the baptism.
2A HUGH LIDDLE, born December 11, 1782.
3 ADAM LIDDLE, born April 2, 1785. Baptized April 22 by Reverend Thomas Romeyn. The Bible records his birth April 22, 1785. Married October 5, 1817, to Melinda Myra Von Crapsey, who was born August 12, 1794, and died November 18, 1866. Adam died October 11, 1877. Both buried at West Shelby, Orleans County, New York. For further reference see Adam Liddle records in this volume.
3A MARGARET LIDDLE, born November 7, 1787.
3B JACOB LIDDLE, born September 18, 1791. Died young, date unknown.
3C DAVID LIDDLE, born July 15, 1793. David had a son William and daughter Jane.
4 JACOB LIDDLE, born November 20, 1795.
4A NANCY LIDDLE, born August 18, 1798.
4B WILLIAM LIDDLE, born July 26, 1801. Bible record year 1800. He returned to Glasgow, Scotland.

Second Generation
John Liddle Branch

JOHN LIDDLE, JR. (2), born Fonda, New York, October 15th or 18th. Baptized there November 12, 1780, by Thomas Romeyn, Pastor of the Reformed Church. Witnesses: John Vrooman and Engeltye (Adaline) Collier. He was married in Fonda, December 20, 1800, to Elizabeth Van Deusen, who was born at Fonda, New York, November 22, 1779, and baptized at Fonda, December 19, 1779, by Reverend Thomas Romeyn.

His wife was the daughter of Gilbert Van Deusen and Nellie Van Antwerp of Johnstown, New York. Gilbert Van Deusen and wife, Nellie Van Antwerp, were first buried at Fultonville, New York, but were removed later and buried in the new part of Greenwood Cemetery, Fonda, New York, on the lot of their grand-daughter, Sarah Caroline Van Deusen Feltis; daughter of Simon Van Deusen and Mary Zimmerman, his wife, who are also buried on same lot.

Gilbert Van Deusen was a Revolutionary soldier and served as sergeant in Captain Garret Putman's Company of Colonel Frederick Fisher's regiment of Tryon County Militia. His certificate number is No. 32720. Gilbert and John Liddle (1) served in the same regiment.

JOHN LIDDLE, JR., resided near Fonda, New York, until about 1823 or 1824 when he took up his residence at Hastings, Oswego County, New York. Elizabeth Van Deusen Liddle, his wife, died Saturday, December 21, 1825. Children 5-13. He died September 26, 1828 and was buried beside his first wife at La Fayette, New York, on the lot of their son Moses. His second marriage was to Miss Newcolm of Syracuse, New York. Two children were born to them 14-15.

Children of John Liddle, Jr. (2) and Elizabeth Van Deusen
Liddle:
These children were all baptized at Fonda, New York, by
Rev. Abraham Van Horne, Pastor of the Reformed Church.

5 JOHN LIDDLE, born Sunday morning, January 10, 1802, at
Fonda, New York. Married at Hastings, New York,
February 16, 1822, to Cathern Ackers. She died August
11, 1848. Buried Branch County, Michigan. Children
16-27. Married again to Roxana Ames, February 28, 1848.
She died April 17, 1874. Children 28-29. Married again to
Helen Wheeler, October 15, 1874, who died October 13,
1911. He died November 11, 1885 at Colon, Michigan.

6 GILBERT LIDDLE, born Friday, December 18, 1803; baptized
January 15, 1804; died January 20, 1806.

7 GILBERT VAN DEUSEN LIDDLE, born Fonda, New York,
Monday, April 7, 1807; baptized 1807; died Tuesday, July
16, 1884. Buried at Colon, Michigan. Married in 1837 to
Julia E. Mathews, who was born 1812; died March 20,
1847. Children 30-32.
Married again to Rebecca Bradley Watson, August 25,
1847, by Reverend Philo Phorbs of the M. E. Church at
Colon, Michigan. She was born near Meadville, Pa.,
Crawford County, August 23, 1825; died July 2, 1910.
She was the daughter of Robert and Martha (Dawson)
Watson of Tionesta, Forest County, Pennsylvania. He
left Hastings, New York, when about 20 years of age and
for three years was employed as a lumberman on the Black
River, Michigan. In 1834 he settled in Colon, Michigan;
purchased from the government 120 acres of land and built
the first brick house in the township. In 1853 he exchanged
this 120 acres for another farm of 500 acres of prairie land
beautifully situated along the St. Joseph River. This farm
was one of the banner farms of the country.
Gilbert Liddle was prominent in his community and highly
respected by all who knew him. He was a member of the
Masonic fraternity and M. E. Church. "Uncle Gill Liddle,"
as he was called, will be remembered for his kindness and
generosity. He gave; not letting his left hand know the

gifts of his right. Many poor received his help never
knowing the identity of their benefactor.

These deeds exemplify the life of this unpretentious man.
He had 9 children and adopted 3 orphans, taking them into
his own household. He died at the age of 77 years. Children
33-38.

8   MOSES LIDDLE was born Wednesday, February 22, 1808;
baptized 1808. Married September 1, 1831 to Andarinda
Wilcox. She was born June 2, 1809; died May 1901; age
92. He died December 28, 1891 at his home in Syracuse,
New York. Both buried at La Fayette, New York. Children 39-41.

9   ELIZA ELEANOR LIDDLE, born Monday, June 18, 1811;
baptized 1811. Married Jacob Madaw. Residence near
Saginaw, Michigan. Child 42.

10   NANCY LIDDLE, born October 1, 1813; baptized 1813; died
January 22, 1877, at Brewerton, New York. Married Hugh
McKinley, who was born November 2, 1811; died April
23, 1897. Children 43-47.

11   MATHEW LIDDLE, born February 13, 1816; baptized 1816;
died in California in 1852 during the gold rush. Supposed
to have been killed by miners for his gold dust. Married
Claricy_____. Married again to Elizabeth Armstrong
Watson, daughter of Robert and Martha (Dawson) Watson.
She was born 1827; died 1848. Buried Colon, Michigan.
Child 48.

12   CATHERN LIDDLE, born November 1, 1818; died March 21,
1898. Married Jacob Young, who was born June 14, 1819;
died May 30, 1899. Both buried at Colby, Wisconsin.
Children 49-53.

13   GETTY (GERTRUDE) MARIE LIDDLE, born December 9, 1822;
died January 11, 1897. Married January 6, 1845 to Frank
Tillman Rhode, who was born January 29, 1817; died January 13, 1897. Both buried in same grave at Constantia,
New York. Residence, Constantia, New York. Child 54.

Children by John Jr. and his second wife, Miss Newcolm:

14   DAVID LIDDLE, born October 4, 1827; drowned when young.
15   WILLIAM LIDDLE, born May 3, 1829.

Third Generation
John Liddle Branch

Children of John Liddle (5) and Elizabeth Ackers:

16 JANE ANN LIDDLE, born February 13, 1823, at Hastings, Oswego County, New York. Residence, Wisconsin.

17 ALVINA B. LIDDLE, born February 17, 1825.

18 FANNIE LIDDLE, born November 30, 1826; died October 18, 1827.

19 HIRUM GILBERT LIDDLE, born June 12, 1828; died 1854 in California. Married Mary Philips. Child 55.

20 PHILO LIDDLE, born October 1, 1830. Married Cynthia Philips. Both buried at Colon, Michigan. Children 56-59.

21 ELIZABETH LIDDLE, born August 9, 1832; died July 13, 1905. Married Timothy Whitmore, who was born March 1, 1832; died October, 1913. Both buried at Colon, Michigan. Children 60-61.

22 CAROLINE LIDDLE, born May 2, 1835; died February 22, 1902. Married George Keyes. Residence, Decatur, Michigan. Both buried there. Children 62-64.

23 JOHN FRANKLIN LIDDLE, born April 16, 1837; died August 4, 1844.

24 CATHERN MARIE LIDDLE, born March 5, 1839; died May 16, 1841.

25 BYRON JACOB LIDDLE, born March 14, 1841; died July 4, 1864. Served as private in the Civil War. Died in the Union Service; buried on the battle-field.

26 HARRIET LIDDLE, born February 23, 1844; died March 12, 1860, age 16.

27 WILLIAM WELLINGTON LIDDLE, born April 7, 1846; died September 8, 1846.

28 Children by second marriage to Roxana Ames. Twins,
29 born and died December 2, 1848.

Children of Gilbert Van Deusen Liddle (7) and Julia Mathews:

30 HENRY MATHEW LIDDLE, born October 15, 1841; died February 28, 1864. Served in Civil War in Company D,

25th Michigan Infantry. Died in Camp at Bowling Green, Kentucky. Buried at Colon, Michigan. Local G. A. R. Post named in his honor.

31 CHARLES MARCELLUS LIDDLE, born January 1, 1842. Married Melinda Leatherberry, of Sherwood, Michigan. Served in Company D, 25th Michigan Infantry. Residence, Loon Lake, Washington. Children 65-68.

32 HARRIET ANN LIDDLE, born January 14, 1844. Married at West Monroe, New York, March 4, 1868, by Reverend J. H. Buck, to Hubbard H. Carr who was born at Haverhill, New Hampshire, February 7, 1837; died Fort Dodge, Kansas. Buried Arkansas City, Kansas, March 15, 1919. Children 69-77.

Children by second marriage to Rebecca Bradley Watson:

33 GILBERT LIDDLE, born December 31, 1848; died September 18, 1913, at Riverside, California. Buried there in Olivewood Cemetery. Graduate of Albion College and of the Law department, University of Michigan. Married December 31, 1874, to Cora Foote of Leonidas, Michigan. She was born October 29, 1855. Child 78.

34 JULIA ELIZABETH LIDDLE, born December 29, 1851; died April 30, 1886. Married George Liddle (56) her second cousin. They are buried at Colon, Michigan. Child 79.

35 MARTHA DAWSON LIDDLE, born Saturday, September 29, 1855. Married at Colon, Michigan, November 25, 1874 to Erastus S. Trubey of Adrian, Ohio, who was born in Crawford County, Ohio, March 16, 1848. Married by Reverend T. T. George, Pastor of the M. E. Church. See Trubey records herein recorded. Children 80-81.

Married again to Pardon Gifford, July 29, 1898, at Vineland, New Jersey, by Reverend Ely Gifford, Pastor of the M. E. Church. Mr. Gifford was born July 29, 1834, at Dartmouth, Massachusetts; died in Vineland, New Jersey, November 10, 1917. Buried Siloam Cemetery. Occupation, retired. Child 82.

36 MARIE HELEN LIDDLE, born March 24, 1857, at Colon, Michigan; died June 18, 1915. Married at Colon, Michigan,

by the Reverend L. B. Tallman, to Frank Freese Welty, who was born at Wilmot, Ohio, December 29, 1854; died March 23, 1915. They resided for a few years at Beach City, Ohio; then moved to Hicksville, Ohio; then to Colon, Michigan. Both buried at Colon, Michigan. Children 83-87.

37 KATHERINE REBECCA LIDDLE, born September 11, 1860. Married at Union City, Michigan, April 14, 1886, by Reverend Orwick to George M. Sides, who was born August 23, 1850 and died July 13, 1921. Residence, Colon, Michigan. Children 88-89.

38 HENRY WATSON LIDDLE, born November 13, 1865. Married Frances Neeley at Coldwater, Kansas, November 8, 1888. Residence, Wellington, Kansas. Children 90-94.

Children of Moses Liddle (8) and Andarinda Wilcox:

39 SARAH LIDDLE, born September 22, 1833; died May 7, 1858.

40 MORRIS LIDDLE, born July 11, 1835. Married in 1861 to Louisa Seever who was born June 11, 1840; died June 28, 1902. He died August 31, 1919. Children 95-96.
Married again Mary Shaw. Residence, Syracuse, New York. Occupation, retired.

41 NOYES LIDDLE, born October 22, 1840. Married January 9, 1862 to Lucinda Rowland, who was born December 9, 1839; died August 18, 1877. Buried La Fayette, New York. Children 97-98.
Married again Myra Smith, born February 19, 1838; died 1915. Residence, Syracuse, New York. Occupation, retired.

Child of Eliza Eleanor Liddle Madaw (9) and Jacob Madaw:

42 WALLACE MADAW, no record, except that he resided in Missouri.

Children of Nancy Liddle (10) and Hugh McKinley:

43 GILBERT LIDDLE McKINLEY, born April 29, 1834; died April 27, 1901. Married November 22, 1860, to Elizabeth Van O Linda, born August 31, 1836; died December 11, 1911. Both are buried at Cisero, New York. Children 99-102.

44 CAROLINE McKINLEY, born January 10, 1837. Married James Strail. Child 103.

Married again Milton Miller; died February, 1916. Residence, Brewerton, New York. Children 104-106.

45 HAYS DUNCAN McKINLEY, born November 11, 1841; died December 27, 1915. Married January 13, 1869, to Charlotte Van Heusen, born March 5, 1843; died January 26, 1914. Residence, Clay, New York and Phoenix, New York. Occupation, farmer. Children 107-110.

46 MARIETTE McKINLEY, born August 27, 1845; died January 19, 1916. Married September 30, 1875, to Charles Moulton, born March 25, 1838. Residence, Brewerton, New York. Child 111.

47 BYRON TILLMAN McKINLEY, born September 1, 1854; died August 23, 1858.

Child of Mathew Liddle (11) and Elizabeth Armstrong Watson:

48 JOHN ROBERT LIDDLE, born April 7, 1848. Residence, Colon, Michigan.

Children of Cathern Liddle (12) and Jacob Young:

49 JAMES K. YOUNG, born May 12, 1846; died in 1864. Served as private in Civil War. Buried in the Southland.

50 EMALINE YOUNG, born March 13, 1841. No record of her family.

51 JACOB YOUNG, born July 5, 1848; died August 5, 1905.

52 MARTHA MARIA YOUNG, born July 20, 1852; died November 29, 1917, at Colby, Wisconsin. Also buried there. Married October 15, 1872, to Moses Adelbert Young; born June 7, 1849. Children 112-116.

53 GILBERT YOUNG, born December 20, 1858; died August 13, 1884.

Child of Getty (Gertrude) Maria Liddle (13) and Frank Tillman Rhode:

54 JENNIE RHODE, born April 11, 1858. Married January 7, 1877, to Edward Slocum. Residence, West Amboy, New York. Occupation, flour and feed merchant. Child 117.

Fourth Generation
John Liddle Branch

Child of Hirum Gilbert Liddle (19) and Mary Philips:

55 FRANKLIN LIDDLE, born October 1, 1852. Married Melinda Hazen. Residence, Colon, Michigan.

Children of Philo Liddle (20) and Cynthia Philips:

56 GEORGE LIDDLE, born 1849. Married Julia Elizabeth Liddle (34). Both buried at Colon, Michigan. Child 79.

57 JOHN LIDDLE, married Nellie Raynor. Both buried at Colon, Michigan.

58 JANE LIDDLE, born July 17, 1876. Married December 2, 1896, to John Sweeder of Leonidas, Michigan. See Index, Children 176-177.

59 VANCE LIDDLE, born June 3, 1874.

Children of Elizabeth Liddle (21) and Timothy Whitmore:

60 LUELLA WHITMORE, born April 19, 1866. Married Harry Mellen. Residence, Colon, Michigan. (See Index, Child 178; also daughter of 178, No. 179 in Index.)

61 SCHUYLER WHITMORE, born June 25, 1868. Married Matilda Schultz. He died in 1919. Buried, Colon, Michigan.

Children of Caroline Liddle (22) and George Keyes:

62 KATHERN A. KEYES, born November 15, 1858; died 1916. Married Fletcher Tanner. Residence, Saratoga, Indiana. Also buried there. Children 118-119.

63 ELY E. KEYES, born May 11, 1860. Married Ella Gardner of Mattison, Michigan. Children 120-121.

64 LILLIAN J. KEYES, born September 4, 1871. Married Edward Fisk of Colon, Michigan. Residence, Leonidas, Michigan. Children 122-123.

Children of Charles Marcellus Liddle (31) and Melinda Leatherberry:

65 RAY LIDDLE, born June 19, 1873, Colon, Michigan. See Index, Children 180-181.

19

66 FRED LIDDLE, born February, 1878, Colon, Michigan. See Index, Children 182-183.

67 FRANK LIDDLE, born July, 1881.

68 ROE LIDDLE, born December, 1886. Residence, Loon Lake, Washington. Children 184-185-186.

Children of Harriet A. Liddle (32) and Hubbard D. Carr:

69 GILBERT H. CARR, born December 19, 1868, at Constantia, Oswego County, New York. Married Edith Carl who was born February 17, 1872. They were married August 29, 1898, at Independence, Missouri. Residence, Kansas City, Missouri.

70 CHARLES F. CARR, born December 25, 1870, at Constantia, New York. Died May 8, 1899, by drowning in the Arkansas River at Ralston, Oklahoma. Also buried there.

71 CARRIE LOUISA CARR, born at Kidder, Missouri, April 11, 1872. Died April 19, 1872.

72 CORA ELOISE CARR, born April 11, 1872; died May 29, 1872. Both buried at Kidder, Missouri.

73 CLINTON H. CARR, born September 25, 1874, at Kidder, Missouri. Married May Taggen who was killed in an automobile accident.

74 MINNIE J. CARR, born May 29, 1877, at Kidder, Missouri. Married at Ralston, Oklahoma, October 12, 1898, to Ona Broadwell, who died April 27, 1912, at Usk, Washington. Married again to Frank Smith, June 1914. Residence, Usk, Washington. Children 124-125.

75 NELLIE MARIE CARR, born March 23, 1880, at Kidder, Missouri. Died June 22, 1911, at Oklahoma City. Buried Arkansas City, Kansas, Riverside Cemetery. Married William F. Hendrix.

76 ARTHUR TILLMAN CARR, born September 20, 1883, at Rhinecliff, New York. Died there February 12, 1884. Also buried there.

77 FREDDIE LIDDLE CARR, born at Cameron, Missouri, March 3, 1886; died Kidder, Missouri, October 23, 1887. Buried there.

Child of Gilbert Liddle, Jr. (33) and Cora Foote:

78 ORLEY ERWIN LIDDLE, born May 25, 1878, at Ellenwood, Kansas. Married at Los Angeles, September 20, 1903, to Blanche Thomas, born December 25, 1878. Residence, Salina, California. Child 126.

Child of Julia Elizabeth Liddle (34) and George Liddle (56):

79 ERNEST PHILO LIDDLE, born February 22, 1881. Residence, Colon, Michigan.

Children of Martha D. Liddle (35) and Erastus S. Trubey. (See Trubey Records):

80 HALLA BELLE TRUBEY, born Tuesday, August 17, 1875, at Beach City, Ohio. Married in Camden, New Jersey, Saturday, August 11, 1906, by the Reverend James T. Bills, to James K. Hirst, who was born September 12, 1877, in Philadelphia, Pennsylvania. Residence, Los Angeles. Children 127-130.

81 VALERIE ANITA TRUBEY, born Tuesday, April 18, 1882, at Colon, Michigan. Married at Vineland, New Jersey, by Reverend David H. King of the Presbyterian Church, June 27, 1906, to William Homer Walker, LL.D., Dean of Desquane University. Mr. Walker was born at Erie, Pennsylvania, September 14, 1883. Residence, Pittsburg, Pennsylvania. Children 131-134.

Child of Martha Liddle (35) and Pardon Gifford:

82 WENDELL PARDON GIFFORD, born July 30, 1900, Monday P. M. in Vineland, New Jersey.

82A MARJORY ROSE MORGAN GIFFORD, adopted daughter. Born September 15, 1905.

Children of Marie Helen Liddle (36) and Frank Freese Welty:

83 HARRY FREESE WELTY, born April 18, 1884, at Beach City, Ohio; died at Hicksville, Ohio, April 14, 1886. Buried Colon, Michigan.

84 GEORGE FRANK WELTY, born January 19, 1886, at Beach City, Ohio. Married July 1, 1913, at Chicago Heights, Illinois, to Susan Marie Stuart who was born April 21, 1890. Residence, Milwaukee, Wisconsin.

85 HELEN FRANCES WELTY, born Hicksville, Ohio, June 22, 1888. Married at Colon, Michigan, January 20, 1913, to George Orla Engle, who was born March 13, 1884. Residence, Colon, Michigan. Children 134A-134B.

86 RUSSELL WARREN WELTY, born Colon, Michigan, March 25, 1895. Died in France, December 18, 1918, of pneumonia while serving in the A. E. F. Body removed to Lakeside Cemetery, Colon, Michigan. The Russell W. Welty post of the American Legion was named in his honor.

87 LOREN AUSTIN WELTY, born Colon, Michigan, October 15, 1897.

Children of Katherine Rebecca Liddle (37) and George M. Sides:

88 RAYMOND M. SIDES, born Colon, Michigan, May 29, 1894. Commissioned in Field Artillery U. S. A. during World War. Residence, Chicago. Occupation, advertising profession.

89 HAROLD ISAAC SIDES, born Colon, Michigan, December 11, 1898.

Children of Henry Watson Liddle (38) and Frances Neeley Liddle:

90 HARRY MAURICE LIDDLE, born Derby, Kansas, October 8, 1890; died December 22, 1891 at Ponca City, Oklahoma. Buried Derby, Kansas.

91 BERTHA HELEN LIDDLE, born Ponca City, Oklahoma, February 12, 1893. Married Howard F. Baker, December 25, 1912. Residence in 1920, Tulsa, Oklahoma. Child 134C.

92 HAROLD WATSON LIDDLE, born Cross, Oklahoma, November 30, 1894; died at Herrington, Kansas, August 21, 1904. Buried at Colon, Michigan.

93 ESTHER LUCILE LIDDLE, born December 7, 1897. Married William A. Phelps, February 8, 1917. Residence, Wellington, Kansas.

94 KENNETH PAUL LIDDLE, born October 20, 1908.

Children of Morris Liddle (40) and Louisa Seever:

95 HERBERT LIDDLE, born January 26, 1862. Married Ella Miller. Residence, Syracuse, New York.

96 CLAYTON LIDDLE, born June, 1866. Married Luella Miller, born 1867. Residence, Syracuse, New York. Child 135.

Children of Noyes Liddle (41) and Lucinda Rowland:
97   ALIDA MAY LIDDLE, born July 23, 1870. Married January 9, 1889 to Joseph H. Abbey. Child 136. Married again March 26, 1905, to William Seeley. Children 137-139.
98   FRANK LYFORD LIDDLE, born January 30, 1873; died April 2, 1915. Married June 21, 1894 to Laura Wadman, who was born December 10, 1875. Residence, Syracuse, New York. Children 140-142.

Children of Gilbert Liddle McKinley (43) and Elizabeth Van O Linda:
99   BION VAN O LINDA McKINLEY, born March 11, 1862. Married August 7, 1893, to Bertha Boynton, born August 2, 1864. Residence, Cisero, New York. Children 143-144.
100 URETTA MAY McKINLEY, born May 6, 1865; died August 4, 1865.
101 EUGENE FRITZ McKINLEY, born July 16, 1866. Married September 10, 1895 to Eva May Crouse, born January 1, 1868. Residence, White Plains, New York. Children 145-146.
102 FLOY OLIVE McKINLEY, born July 15, 1877. Married July 26, 1893 to Rodney S. Miller, born September 10, 1871. Residence, Brewerton, New York. Children 147-150.

Child of Caroline McKinley (44) and James Strail:
103 JAMES M. STRAIL.

Children of Caroline McKinley (44) and Milton Miller:
104 MABEL S. MILLER, born October 7, 1866; died March 16, 1887, age 21 years.
105 MINER MILLER, born August 1869. Married Lizzie Stier. Residence, Courtland, New York. Child 151.
106 JUDSON MILLER, born January 18, 1871. Married October 25, 1890 to Jennie Schoolcraft, born October 26, 1870. Residence, Syracuse, New York. Children 152-154.

Children of Hays Duncan McKinley (45) and Charlotte Van Heusen:
107 NELLIE ESTELLE McKINLEY, born October 29, 1872; died September 27, 1877.
108 FRED CLAUD McKINLEY, born March 2, 1877. Married

Grace Pearl Edgerton, January 4, 1904. Residence, Minoa, New York. Children 155-156.

109 FLORENCE IDA McKINLEY, born October 28, 1880. Married January 20, 1904 to George Edward Booth, born March 5, 1868. Residence, Phoenix, New York. Child 157.

110 JESSIE PEARL McKINLEY, born September 20, 1883; died November 18, 1910. Married June 15, 1900 to Edward Kenyon. Residence, Euclid, New York. Children 158-161.

Child of Mariette McKinley (46) and Charles Moulton:

111 GLEN MOULTON, born April 19, 1878. Married May Everson. Residence, Brewerton, New York. Children 162-165.

Children of Martha Young (52) and Moses Adelbert Young:

112 WALLACE FRANKLIN YOUNG, born May 9, 1874. Married November 21, 1904 at Spokane, Washington, Union Park M. E. Church, by Reverend M. R. Brown, to Agnes Gottschoek Robenhorst, born May 2, 1871.

113 ETTA MAY BELLE YOUNG, born November 20, 1876. Married at Colby, Wisconsin, August 19, 1897 by Reverend S. A. Hoffman, to John J. Grimes who was born May 25, 1871. Residence, Colby, Wisconsin. Occupation, retired merchant.

114 CATHERN BORENA YOUNG, born July, 1884. Married June 4, 1914 at Spokane, Washington, by Reverend John J. Heam, to Franklin W. Peterson, born April 20, 1881. Child 165A.

115 BEULA ORA YOUNG, born June 7, 1887. Married May 12, 1906 at Colby, Wisconsin, by Reverend James, to Charles Schultz. Children 166-167.

116 JACOB ADELBERT YOUNG, born August 13, 1892. Principal of High School at Colby, Wisconsin. Enlisted U. S. A. July, 1917. Embarked for France, February, 1918, as Medical Superintendent 121st Field Artillery, 32nd Division.

Child of Jennie Rhode (54) and Edward Slocum:

117 HARRY D. SLOCUM, born July 18, 1883. Married December 31, 1907 to Ethel Weaver, born November 14, 1886. Residence, West Amboy, New York. Child 168.

Fifth Generation
John Liddle Branch

Children of Kathern A. Keyes (62) and Fletcher Tanner:

118   GERTRUDE E. TANNER, born November 20, 1880; died January 23, 1901 at Saratoga, Indiana.

119   GEORGE KEYES TANNER, born June 8, 1883. Residence, Saratoga, Indiana. Unmarried.

Children of Ely E. Keyes (63) and Ella Gardner:

120   HAZEL IRENE KEYES, born July 28, 1888. Married Robert D. Menzel. Residence, Washington, D. C.

121   IVAN GARDNER KEYES, born November 19, 1889. Residence, Colon, Michigan.

Children of Lillian J. Keyes (64) and Edward Fisk:

122   HOLLY KEYES FISK, born March 10, 1892. Married Pearl Prescot, born March 4, 1889. Residence, Flint, Michigan. Children 169-170.

123   E. JUANITA FISK, born May 26, 1894. Married Henry D. Miller. Residence, Constantine, Michigan. Children 171-173.

Children of Minnie J. Carr (74) and Ona Broadwell:

123A ERNEST EARL BROADWELL, born October 29, 1899; died young.

124   OPAL AGNES BROADWELL, born August 2, 1901 at Ralston, Oklahoma (Pawnee County). Residence, Usk, Washington.

125   PEARL NELLIE BROADWELL, born March 23, 1903 at Ralston, Oklahoma.

Child of Orley Erwin Liddle (78) and Blanche Thomas:

126   GLADYS EILEEN LIDDLE, born August 21, 1904. Residence, Salina, California.

Children of Halla Belle Trubey (80) and James K. Hirst:

The children were baptized at St. Andrews Episcopal

Church, March 14, 1917, at Los Angeles, California.

127 DELELLE EDGAR HIRST, born Easter April 19, 1908 at Vineland, New Jersey. Died May 5, 1918 at Los Angeles, California.

128 MARTHA HELENE HIRST, born Saturday, August 27, 1910 at Los Angeles, California.

129 JAMES VINCENT HIRST, born Sunday, October 30, 1912 at Los Angeles, California.

130 HALLA LAVEDA HIRST, born March 14, 1915 at Los Angeles, California.

Children of Valerie Anita Trubey (81) and William Homer Walker:

131 WILLIAM HOMER WALKER, JR., born Sunday morning May 12, 1907 at Erie, Pennsylvania.

131A VALERIE ELIZABETH (BETTY) WALKER, born Erie, Pennsylvania, November 10, 1908; died January 6, 1919 at Pittsburg, Pennsylvania. Buried at Erie, Pennsylvania.

131B MARTHA MAY WALKER, born November 20, 1909 at North East, Pennsylvania, died at Erie, Pennsylvania, March 8, 1913. Buried at Erie, Pennsylvania.

132 ROBERT VAN DEUSEN WALKER, born Crafton Heights, Pittsburg, Pennsylvania, November 26, 1917. 210 Earl Avenue.

133 FRANCIS JOHN WALKER, born at 141 Stratford Avenue, E. End Pittsburg, Pennsylvania, March 20, 1919.

134 JOSEPH HENRY WALKER, born September 29, 1920, at 141 Stratford Ave., E. End, Pittsburg, Pennsylvania.

Children of Helen Frances Welty (85) and George Orla Engle:

134A MARIE LORENE ENGLE, born August 22, 1918; died September 12, 1918 at Colon, Michigan.

134B RUSSELL GEORGE ENGLE, born September 19, 1919 at Colon, Michigan.

Child of Bertha Helen Liddle (91) and Howard F. Baker:

134C FRANCES LUCILE BAKER, born at Ponca City, Oklahoma, October 1, 1914.

Child of Clayton Liddle (96) and Luella Miller:

135 OLIVER LONGSTREET LIDDLE, born 1894.

Child of Alida May Liddle (97) and Joseph H. Abbey:

136 CORA LUELLA ABBEY, born March 28, 1890. Married July 4, 1906 to Hever Featherstone. Children 174-175.

Children of Alida May Liddle (97) and Eugene Seeley:

137 LUCINDA MAY SEELEY, born March 1, 1906.
138 FLORENCE EUGENE SEELEY, born January 5, 1908.
139 FLOYD NOYES LIDDLE SEELEY, born December, 1909; died February 13, 1910.

Children of Frank Lyford Liddle (98) and Laura Olive Wadman:

140 INEZ RUTH LIDDLE, born March 4, 1895. Married Edmund Tiller August 26 or 27, 1917. Residence, Springfield, Mass.
141 EARL ROWLAND LIDDLE, born June 14, 1900.
142 CLARENCE B. LIDDLE, born August 22, 1901.

Children of Bion Van O Linda McKinley (99) and Bertha Boynton:

143 GILBERT ROSS McKINLEY, born August 31, 1894; died May 12, 1897.
144 REED McKINLEY, born August 31, 1902.

Children of Eugene Fritz McKinley (101) and Eva May Crouse:

145 MARJORIE CROUSE McKINLEY, born October 16, 1898.
146 WILLIAM McKINLEY, born October 8, 1903.

Children of Floy Olive McKinley (102) and Rodney S. Miller:

147 HOBART McKINLEY MILLER, born June 23, 1896.
148 MARCIA BELLE McKINLEY MILLER, born April 9, 1899.
149 CYREL CLAUD MILLER, born February 3, 1901.
150 KENNETH KARL MILLER, born February 15, 1906.

Child of Miner Miller (105) and Lizzie Stier:

151 CARL MILLER.

Children of Judson Miller (106) and Jennie Schoolcraft:

152 GARDNER MILLER, born February 2, 1899.
153 MABEL MILLER, born July 9, 1895.
154 JUDSON NATHAN MILLER, born September 8, 1897.

Children of Fred McKinley (108) and Grace Pearl Edgerton:

155 JOHN HAYS MCKINLEY, born April 22, 1905.

156 RICHARD STEPHEN MCKINLEY, born March 9, 1907.

Child of Florence McKinley (109) and Edward Booth:

157 CHARLOTTE AMY BOOTH, born January 7, 1907.

Children of Jessie Pearl McKinley (110) and Edward Kenyon:

158 LE ROY OAKLEY KENYON, born June 7, 1901.

159 MARTHA ARLEEN KENYON, born September 1, 1902.

160 EDWARD H. FAY KENYON, born July 13, 1904.

161 JESSIE OLETA KENYON, born November 17, 1910; died December 20, 1910.

Children of Glen Moulton (111) and May Everson:

162 EARL MOULTON, born January 5, 1908.

163 WALTER MOULTON, born January 9, 1910.

164 REXFORD MOULTON, born October 6, 1911.

165 ANNA MOULTON, born July 30, 1915. Residence, Brewerton, New York.

Child of Cathern Borena Young (114) and Franklin W. Peterson:

165A ARNOLD ADELBERT PETERSON, born September 11, 1918.

Children of Beula Ora Young (115) and Charles Schultz:

166 ERMA MAY SCHULTZ, born November 6, 1907 at Colby, Wisconsin.

167 EDWARD SCHULTZ, born August 22, 1910 at Colby, Wisconsin.

Child of Harry D. Slocum (117) and Ethel Weaver:

168 MARION JEANETT SLOCUM, born December 1, 1908, at West Amboy, New York.

Sixth Generation
John Liddle Branch

Children of Holly Keyes Fisk (122) and Pearl Prescot:

169 PALMER K. FISK, born May 5, 1914; died May 9, 1914.

170 DOROTHY AILEEN FISK, born February 5, 1916.

Children of E. Juanita Fisk (123) and Harry D. Miller:

171 WILLIAM F. MILLER, born August 20, 1913.

172 CHARLES HOLLY MILLER, born August 4, 1914.

173 EDWARD D. MILLER, born June 3, 1916.

Children of Cora Luella Abbey (136) and Hever Featherstone:

174 NORMAN FREDENE FEATHERSTONE, born August 3, 1908.

175 FRANCES LEONA FEATHERSTONE, born July 7, 1909.

* * * * *

The following records were received too late to be classified in regular order and are therefore assigned numbers beginning with 176.

Children of Jane Liddle (58) and John Sweeder:

176 CHARLES SWEEDER, born May 24, 1901.

177 LEO VANCE SWEEDER, born November 15, 1906.

Child of Luella Whitmore (60) and Harry Mellen:

178 WAIVE LORANE MELLEN, born July 23, 1892. Married July 29, 1908 to George H. Moulton. They had one child.

Child of Waive Mellen (178) and George Moulton:

179 MADELENE MAY MOULTON, born November 1, 1911, at Dailey, Michigan.

Children of Ray Liddle (65). Had two children (daughters):

180 One born 1904.

181 One born 1907.

Children of Fred Liddle (66):

182 EDNA AILEEN LIDDLE, born 1906.

183 MELBOURN HOWARD LIDDLE, born 1911.

Van Doersen

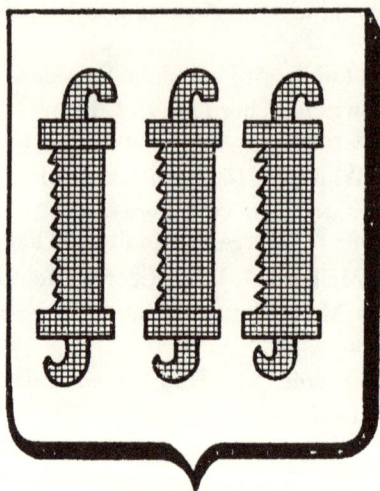

Van Antwerpen

The Van Deusen Family Records

This family is connected with the John Liddle, Jr. 2 family. Albert II. Van Deusen has prepared two volumes of history covering that family. For the benefit of the John Liddle, Jr. 2 lineage they are copied by permission.

The Van Deusen family came from Holland. The first record we have of this family is Hendricus A. Doersen (Henry Van Doersen) born 1196.

1325   GOVERT VAN DOORSEN.

1325   JAN III. DUKE OF BRABANT.

1325   DUCHESS JOHANNA, third daughter of Jan III, who died in 1406 from her son Jan. There is no break in the records.

1st Gen.   JAN VAN DEURSEN, great or great-great-grandson of
1406   Govert Van Doorsen. Married Aleid (Adaline) Van Bloemenseerde. Their son:

2nd Gen.   JAN (JOHN) VAN DEURSEN, married Aleid (Adaline) Dompselear. Their son:

3rd Gen.   JAN VAN DEURSEN II, married Wilhelmina Zoudenbalg.

4th Gen.   NICOLAS VAN DEURSEN, son of Jan II, married Machteld (Matilda) Procys.

5th Gen.   JAN WILLEM VAN DEURSEN, son of Nicolas, married the daughter of Gerritt (Gerald) Heusden.

6th Gen.   JAN VAN DEURSEN, son of Jan Willem, married Elizabeth Van Heusden. This Jan was living in 1550 and was the last male descendant of Govert Van Doorsen who held the ancestral seat the lands and Castle of Deursen. Both his mother and wife were from the old and renowned house of Heusden. His son:

7th Gen.   HENDRICK (HENRY) was born in the old Castle. He married Maria Rutgers and had one son:

8th Gen. WILLEM VAN DEURSEN, who married Elizabeth Gysbert (Gilbert). Their son:

9th Gen. PIETER VAN DEURSEN, (wife no record) became magistrate of Haerlem, Holland, in 1583. His son:

10th Gen. ABRAHAM (PIETERSEN) VAN DEURSEN was born in Haerlem, Holland. Baptized there November 11, 1607. Married there December 9, 1629 to Tryntje (Cathern) Melchiors, also of Haerlem. Soon after their marriage they emigrated to New Amsterdam (now New York City). His house or property was the third lot south of Wall Street, opposite Trinity Church. It was there that he maintained the English soldiers in 1665. They were members of the Dutch Reformed Church. They had six children. He was a miller by occupation. This Abraham (Pietersen) Van Deursen and wife, Tryntje Melchiors, are our first American ancestors and represent the 10th generation from Holland. Their oldest son:

11th Gen. TEUWIS (MATTHEWS) (ABRAHAMSEN) VAN DEURSEN, is the 11th generation from Holland and 1st in America, born 1631. Married Helena Robberts in 1653. This family removed from New York City to Beverwyck (Albany). Was granted a lot October 28, 1658. Lived there until 1700. He also resided in Claverack, New York. They had 11 children. Their son:

12th Gen. JACOBUS is the 12th generation from Holland and 2nd in America, and is the 6th child of (Teuwis). Married November 14, 1695, to Aeltje (Alice) Gysbertse (Gilberts) Uytenbogaert. He died before 1729. She died September 3, 1731. She was the daughter of Dirck Uytenbogaert and Lysbeth Eckerson (Pioneer families of New York City). They have 7 children. Their fifth child:

13th Gen. GYSBERT (GILBERT) VAN DEURSEN is the 13th generation from Holland and 3rd in America. Gysbert was baptized April 23, 1704. Married May 14, 1726 to Hanna Ten Broeck. She was the daughter of Andries Ten Broeck and Lyntje (Lena) Splinters. Residence, New York City. Occupation, mason. They had 11 children.

14th Gen. ANDRIES VAN DEUSEN, is the 14th generation from Holland and 4th in America, baptized June 9, 1728. Married April 24, 1751, to Elizabeth Ute (Ott). They had 6 children, all baptized in New York City. Their second child:

15th Gen. GYSBERT (GILBERT) being the 15th generation from Holland and 5th in America. He was born March 7, 1755. Baptized March 13, 1755; died July 15, 1832. Married October 19, 1775 at Fonda, Montgomery County, New York, by Reverend Thomas Romine (Romeyn), Pastor of the Reformed Church, to Neeltje (Nellie) Van Antwerp of Johnstown, New York, who was born 1761; died October 23, 1833. See Van Antwerp records herein recorded.

They are both buried in Greenwood Cemetery in the new part, on the lot of their granddaughter, Sarah Caroline Van Deusen Feltis; wife of Josiah Feltis and daughter of Simon Van Deusen and Mary Zimmerman. This Gilbert Van Deusen was a Sergeant in Captain Garret Putman's Company of Colonel Frederick Fisher's Regiment. His certificate number is 32720. Reference: New York State Library, where the Revolutionary records are preserved. They had 13 children.

16th Gen. from Holland and 6th in America is ELIZABETH VAN DEUSEN, daughter of Gilbert and Nellie (Van Antwerp) Van Deusen. She was their third child. With Elizabeth, the Van Deusen name ends, she having married John Liddle, Jr., December 20, 1800. This John Liddle, Jr. 2 is the son of our first American ancestor, John Liddle.

See John Liddle 2 Records for further record of Elizabeth Van Deusen.

Trubey Family Records

This family is connected with the Liddle records through (35) of the John Branch. Daniel Trubey, Sr., and wife Maue (Maw) came to America from Hesse Castle (Land Grave) in Germany and settled in Washington County, Maryland.

Daniel Trubey, Jr., son of Daniel and Maue Trubey, married Mary Stoner. She was the daughter of David Stoner of Waynesboro, Franklin County, Pennsylvania. A deed made to David and Abraham Stoner in 1747 in Franklin County, near Waynesboro, is in the possession of Mrs. Snively, a descendant. J. J. Oler, of Waynesboro, has the records.

David Trubey, son of Daniel, Jr., was one of eleven children and married Keziah Klinker of Barr's Mills, now Beach City, Ohio. They had four children.

Erastus Seabery Trubey, son of David Trubey, born March 26, 1848, at Adrian, Ohio, married Martha Liddle, November 25, 1874, at Colon, Michigan. Had two children, Halla Belle and Valerie Anita.

Von Crapser Family Records

The name was changed to Crapsey. John Von Crapser came from Germany and settled with the Puritans in New York.

Rev. Jacob Von Crapsey—born May 2, 1767—died November 8, 1832. His wife, Anna Griffith (English descent) was born August 15, 1767—died January 21, 1847. Their Children:

1. Mary Crapsey   Born December 13, 1789
2. John G. Crapsey   Born January 27, 1791
3. Ayubah Crapsey   Born February 8, 1792
4. Melinda Myra Crapsey   Born August 12, 1794
5. Daniel W. Crapsey   Born February 14, 1797
6. Nancy Crapsey   Born July 22, 1799
7. Moses C. Crapsey   Born March 11, 1802
8. Tryphosa Crapsey   Born September 16, 1804
9. Jacob Crapsey   Born March 27, 1808

Melinda Myra Crapsey (4) was the wife of Adam Liddle (3).

The Van Antwerpen Family Records

Extract from "*Hudson and Mohawk Valleys*," page 972

"Danielse Janse VanAntwerpen born in 1635 son of Jan (John) from Holland. In 1650 he was deputy schout fiscal at Fort Orange (Albany). September 1661 he agreed with Adrian Appel who was an inn-keeper in New Amsterdam and trader in Albany to serve him in all matters and affairs that are just and right for one year in consideration of the sum of thirty-five beavers, one hundred and twelve dollars $112.00 and all expense. Soon after Schenectady was settled (about 1670) he became possessed of the third flat on the south side of the Mohawk river about eight miles above Schenectady. In 1706 he sold the west half of his bowery (63 a, 79 rods) to his neighbor, Jan Pieterse Mabie. In 1676 he was one of the five magistrates; in 1701 supervisor of the town."

Extract from "*Hudson and Mohawk Valleys*," page 412

"The family name of VanAntwerp has this significance through the Dutch: that the family to which this cognomen was applied resided near the wharf, tying up the ships, and in this sense also it could signify that before they took up residence in Holland or emigrated to America, they came from the great seaport of Belgium, Antwerp, the capital of the province of the same name."

1st Gen. JAN (JOHN) from Antwerp, Holland.

2nd Gen. DANIEL JANSE VAN ANTWERPEN, son of Jan (John) from Antwerp, Holland. He was born in 1635 at Beverwyck, New York; married Maria Groot. daughter of Simon Groot and Rebecca DeTrieux. They had eight children.

3rd Gen. ARENT DANIELSE, the third child of Daniel Janse Van Antwerpen and Maria Groot. He married Sara VanEps, daughter of Johannes VanEps.

4th Gen. NEELTJE (NELLIE) VANANTWERPEN, daughter of
Arent Danielse VanAntwerpen and Sara VanEps.
She was baptized April 28th, 1710, in Albany, New
York and married her cousin, Harmanus Van
Antwerpen.

5th Gen. JOHANNES VAN ANTWERP, son of Neeltje and
Harmanus VanAntwerpen, baptized Feb. 6th, 1732.
He married Annetje (Anna) Veeder March 4th, 1755.

6th Gen. NEELTJE (NELLIE) VAN ANTWERP, daughter of
Johannes and Annetje (Anna) Veeder Van Antwerp
was born in 1761; married at Fonda, New York,
Montgomery Co., October 19th, 1775, to Gilbert
Van Deusen, who was baptized March 13th, 1754
or 1755; he died July 15th, 1832. She died Oct. 23rd,
1833. Both buried at Fonda, New York.

7th Gen. ELISABETH VAN DEUSEN, daughter of Gilbert Van
Deusen and Neeltje (Nellie) Van Antwerp. She was
born November 22nd, baptized December 19th, 1779,
at Fonda, New York. Married John Liddle, Jr., (2)
of the (John Liddle Branch), Dec. 20, 1800.

Watson Family Records

1 JOHN WATSON, whose father's name was Robert, came to
America from North Ireland, though born in Scotland,
and settled in Maryland; married Rebecca Bradley of
Delaware, August 4, 1794, (she was the daughter of Bradley
born in Scotland, and his wife, Margaret Moody, of Wales,
came to America and settled in Delaware).

2 ROBERT WATSON, son of John Watson and Rebecca
Bradley, who was born May 11, 1800, died at Colon,
Michigan, November 17, 1884. He was married to
Martha Dawson, daughter of James Dawson and Eliza-
beth (Armstrong) Dawson, who came from Scotland and
settled in Harrisburg, Pennsylvania, where Martha
Dawson was born October, 1798. She died August 25,
1856. Both are buried at Colon, Michigan. Their eldest
daughter, Rebecca Bradley Watson, married Gilbert
Van Deusen Liddle (7). See John Liddle, Jr., records.

Robert Liddle (16) above, and Alexander Liddle (42) below, both
of the Robert Liddle branch

Charles Liddle (46) and his wife Abigail (White) Liddle of the
Robert Liddle branch

First Generation

Robert Liddle Branch

The Robert Liddle Records were furnished through the courtesy of Frances Mary (Liddle) Fideler (120).

1 ROBERT LIDDLE, born 1741; died September 7, 1822. Elizabeth, his wife, born 1746; died October 15, 1814. Both were born in Roxburghshire, Scotland and came to America in 1775 from New Castleton, Roxburghshire, Scotland, near Sir William Johnstone's Estate "Westerhall," Langholm. This Robert Liddle is a brother of John Liddle, 1, who settled in Fonda, Montgomery County, New York; while Robert settled in the town of Princeton, Schenectady County, New York. Robert built a stone house on his farm which is still occupied (1921), and is known as the Robert Kelly farm. He was a stone mason by trade and constructed some of the first walls laid in Albany traveling many miles through the wilderness to reach his employment.

Robert and his wife came to America with four children, Elizabeth (Betty) was born on the voyage. Robert and wife, with four of their children are buried at Duanesburg, New York. Thomas, John and Alexander with their wives, Christy Liddle Macy, her husband John Macy and their daughter are also buried there. Children 2-8.

Children of Robert Liddle and wife Elizabeth:

2 THOMAS LIDDLE, born 1768 in Scotland; died March 24, 1858. Married Janet Robinson who was born 1772; died February 13, 1875, age 103. Both buried at Duanesburg, New York. Children 9-15.

3 MARGARET LIDDLE, born in Scotland 1771; died July 24, 1849. Married John McCumpha.

4 CHRISTY LIDDLE, born in Scotland 1773; died October 15, 1860. Married John Macy. Both buried at Duanesburg, New York.

5 ELIZABETH (BETTY) LIDDLE, born on voyage over in 1775. Married a brother of her sister Margaret's husband, a McCumpha. They moved to New Fane in western New York. We have no record of their family only that they changed their name to McNeil.

6 ALEXANDER LIDDLE, born 1777; died March 12, 1867. Married Mary Gifford, born 1780; died January 2, 1851. Both buried at Duanesburg, New York. Children 16-24.

7 JANETTE LIDDLE. Married Coulter.

8 JOHN LIDDLE, born 1783; died February 4, 1875. Married Nancy Robinson, born 1786; died September 17, 1854. Buried Duanesburg, New York. Children 25-26.

Second Generation
Robert Liddle Branch

Children of Thomas Liddle (2) and wife Janet Robinson:

9 ALEXANDER LIDDLE, born August 10, 1807; died April 1882. Married in 1838 to Eleanor Blood who was born August 31, 1817; died June, 1886. Residence, Eaton Corners, New York. Buried in Minaville, New York. Children 27-34.

10 ROBERT LIDDLE, Residence, Albion, Orleans County, New York.

11 PETER LIDDLE, Residence, Michigan.

12 JOHN LIDDLE, Residence, Duanesburg, New York.

13 ROMEYN LIDDLE, Buried Duanesburg, New York. Child 35.

14 JANE LIDDLE, born Duanesburg, New York, 1814; died 1904. Married Henry Wright. Residence, Duanesburg, New York. Children 36-41.

15 ELIZABETH LIDDLE, Married Clark Patterson. Residence, Duanesburg, New York.

Children of Alexander Liddle (6) and Mary Gifford:

16 ROBERT LIDDLE, born in Princeton, New York, January 12, 1803; died August 25, 1890, age 87 years. Married three times. First to Sarah Smith, born 1803; died 1843. Second marriage October 6, 1844, to Sarah Robinson who was born 1811; died August 12, 1854. Third marriage in 1857 to

Janet Young, born 1807; died July 19, 1894. She was the daughter of James Young, a pioneer of Schenectady County, New York, who built and operated for years one of the first paper mills in eastern New York. She was a member of the Reformed Presbyterian Church for many years, her father being ruling Elder in the same church. She was a woman of strong and excellent character, widely known and highly respected. Children 42-52B.

17 Thomas Liddle, born 1804; died February 25, 1861. Unmarried.

18 Alexander Liddle, born August 4, 1806; died August 15, 1863. Married Cathern Allen of Princeton, New York, born September 12, 1810; died October 26, 1871. Residence, Duanesburg, New York. Children 53-62.

19 Ann Liddle, born 1808; died March 25, 1867. Married John McMillan. Children 63-68.

20 John Liddle, born February 10, 1812; died November 1, 1883. Married March 10, 1836, Maranda Wright who died February 6, 1897. Children 69-75.

21 William Liddle, born April 14, 1814; died February 24, 1892. Married Delia Fuller, born December 28, 1820; died April 12, 1909. Children 76-77.

22 James Liddle, born June 20, 1815; died September 15, 1897. Married Maria Vanderpool. Children 77A-77B.

23 Mary Liddle, born July 15, 1819; died April 4, 1889. Married January 20, 1848, Alexander D. Jones, born August 10, 1818; died May 15, 1897. Children 78-83.

24 Jane Elizabeth Liddle, unmarried.

Children of John Liddle (8) and Nancy Robinson:

25 Robert Duncan Liddle, born October 9, 1824; died July 2, 1865. Married his second cousin Abigail Liddle (43), daughter of (16). She is still living at Duanesburg, New York (1920). Children 84-87.

26 William Liddle, born August 18, 1829, in Princeton, Schenectady County, New York. Died same place June 12, 1875. Married his second cousin Mary Liddle (44), daughter of (16). She was born August 31, 1830. Died at Gilbert, Story County, Iowa, December 21, 1914. Children 88-96.

Third Generation

Robert Liddle Branch

Children of Alexander Liddle (9) and Eleanor Blood:

27 THOMAS LIDDLE, born January 28, 1839. Married Anna
Runkle who was born January 14, 1845. Residence,
Amsterdam, New York. Children 2 daughters, no record
being available.

28 STEWART BLOOD LIDDLE, born October 5, 1840; died
November, 1866. Had four sons, Robert, Alexander,
William H. and Stewart Blood. All died young.

29 MARY ELIZABETH LIDDLE, born July 18, 1845. Married
John Fletcher Ernest. Children 97-100.

30 SARAH MARGARET LIDDLE, born January 3, 1850. Married
Richard D. Schuyler. Married again, James H. Bronson.
No living children.

31 JEANETTE R. LIDDLE, born May 27, 1852; died April 14,
1877. Married George Serviss. Child 101.

32 JOHN LIDDLE, born January 10, 1854. Married Anna Belle
Ashton. No children.

33 ROBERT BLOOD LIDDLE, born May 19, 1856.

34 IDA MARIE LIDDLE, born March 3, 1863. Married Harry
Sherbourn. Child 102.

Child of Romeyn Liddle (13):

35 JAMES S. LIDDLE. A brush manufacturer. Had several
children the records of whom are unavailable. Residence,
Lockport, New York.

Children of Jane (Liddle) Wright (14) and Henry Wright:

36 JOHN WRIGHT, Residence, Duanesburg, New York.

37 JANE E. WRIGHT, married McDougal.

38 HENRY R. WRIGHT, married Emma Morgan. Occupation,
commission merchant, Albany, New York. Child 103.

39 THOMAS WRIGHT, died 1904.

40 ROBERT WRIGHT, no record.

41 EDWARD WRIGHT, Naoma Furgeson.

Children of Robert Liddle (16) and Sarah Smith:

This Robert Liddle was a member of the Reformed Presbyterian Church established in 1804. The land and cemetery were given by James Duane. A Sabbath School was opened in 1834 of which Robert Liddle was Superintendent for 33 years. This church society first worshipped in the woods, and later in the barns of Walter Maxwell and Robert Liddle. They held services at eleven o'clock, then would have dinner outside from lunch baskets. They called it intermission. Then at one o'clock communion would be taken. A few years after, services were held in a stone church at Princeton.

42   ALEXANDER LIDDLE, born 1827. Married first Barbary Gregg. Children 104-105. Married again Margaret (Crowell) Passage, widow of John Passage. Child 106. He was living at Duanesburg, New York, in 1920.

43   ABIGAIL LIDDLE, born 1828. Married a cousin Robert Duncan Liddle (25). He was born October 9, 1824; died July 2, 1865. They were married January 10, 1849. She was living in 1920 at Duanesburg, New York. See (25) for line.

44   MARY LIDDLE, born August 31, 1830, at Duanesburg, New York; died December 21, 1914, at Gilbert, Story County, Iowa. She was married January 3, 1856, to her second cousin, William Liddle (26), son of (8). He was born August 18, 1829, in Princeton, New York; died there June 12, 1875. See (26) for lineage.

45   ANN ELIZABETH LIDDLE, born March 3, 1834, at Duanesburg, New York; died March 6, 1907. Married January 11, 1855, to George Thomas McFarlan who was born January 11, 1831. Children 107-113.

46   CHARLES LIDDLE, born March 12, 1836; died November 18, 1903. Married February 5, 1836, to Abigail White, born January 15, 1836; died April 10, 1914. This Charles Liddle is the father of Frances Liddle (120) who contributed the records of the Robert branch.

47   THOMAS GIFFORD LIDDLE, born July 18, 1838. Married December 27, 1865, to Mary Jane McFarlan who was born August 22, 1845; died March 28, 1912. They were married

by the Reverend Andrew Gifford Wylie. Served in the Civil War. Enlisted at Duanesburg, New York, August 22, 1862. Discharged at Albany, New York, June 22, 1865. Served in the 134th New York Infantry, Co. H.

48   ABRAM S. LIDDLE, born 1840. Married Mary Ann Vanderpool. Residence, Ames, Iowa. No children. Civil War veteran. Enlisted 12th New York Independence Battery Light Artillery. Artillery Brigade 3rd A. C. Mustered out at Albany, New York, June 25, 1865.

49   ROBERT WILLIAM LIDDLE, born April 30, 1842. Married December 22, 1868, Adalaid Augusta Dix who died March 27, 1914. Children 128A-131A. Married again November 18, 1915, at Scranton, Pennsylvania, to Margaret Louisa Wylie, born at Duanesburg, New York, April 11, 1846. Residence, Regent Park, Tacoma, Washington.

Children of Robert Liddle (16) and second wife, Sarah Robinson:

50   ANGUS MCDERMIT LIDDLE, born January 29, 1846; died March 28, 1917. Married October 20, 1875, to Anna Elizabeth Smith, born December 20, 1853. Children 129-131.

51   DUNCAN ROBINSON LIDDLE, born March 26, 1848; died February 16, 1850.

52   JEANETTE LIDDLE, born August 12, 1850; died May 8, 1904. Twins.

52A   JOHN E. LIDDLE, born April 23, 1853; died September 16, 1855.

52B   SARAH C. LIDDLE, born April 23, 1853; died March, 1858.

Children of Alexander Liddle (18) and Cathern S. Allen of Princeton, New York:

53   ALEXANDER THOMAS LIDDLE, born 1832; died August 1, 1853.

54   WILLIAM ALLEN LIDDLE, born December 15, 1833; died January 28, 1912.

55   ROBERT JAMES LIDDLE, born October 27, 1836; died October, 25, 1916. Married Jane Dunning. Children 132-136.

56   LEAH JEANETTE LIDDLE, born March 13, 1839 at Duanesburg, New York; died November 20, 1914. Married John

Ingersoll, born September 21, 1831, at Clarkston, New York; died July 5, 1873. Children 137-140.

57 MARGARET ISABELLE LIDDLE, born December 24, 1841.
58 JOHN AUGUSTUS LIDDLE, born December 22, 1842.
59 MARY HELEN LIDDLE, born January 24, 1843.
60 ELIZABETH AMELIA LIDDLE, born February 13, 1844. Married January, 1871, to William J. McClure who was born March 29, 1842. Child 141.
61 THOMAS EDWARD LIDDLE, born August 24, 1854. Married December 20, 1874, to Melinda Auchampaugh who was born August 28, 1864. Residence, Knox, Albany County, New York.
62 SARAH CATHERN LIDDLE, born June, 1856.

Children of Ann Alizabeth Liddle (19) and John McMillan:

63 ANDREW THOMAS McMILLAN, born November 27, 1832. Married March 12, 1868, to Cathern Elizabeth McMillan. Children 141A-141B.
64 JOHN ALEXANDER McMILLAN, born March 3, 1836.
65 JAMES McMILLAN, born May 20, 1838. Unmarried.
66 ROBERT McMILLAN, born December 9, 1842.
67 BENJAMIN McMILLAN, born April 17, 1848. Married Elizabeth M. Stillwell. Children 141C-141E. Married again Mary L. Stillwell (sister of his first wife) April 18, 1883. Children 141F-141G.
68 MARY JANE McMILLAN, born January 3, 1855. Married John F. Clogston. She died June 28, 1918.

Children of John Liddle (20) and Maranda Wright. Their children were all born in Duanesburg, New York:

69 ALEXANDER LIDDLE, born May 27, 1838; died September 21, 1839.
70 MARY CATHERN LIDDLE, born October 14, 1840; died July 17, 1844.
71 GEORGE THOMAS LIDDLE, born May 10, 1843; died in Schenectady, New York, November 18, 1914. Married April 25, 1865, to Lydia Vanderpool. She died November 10, 1910. Children 142-146.
72 WILLIAM HENRY LIDDLE, born June 19, 1845; died Septem-

ber 23, 1898. Married Zelphina Jane Knapp on June 19,
1866. She died September, 1887. Children 147-151.
Married again October, 1889, to Lucretia Jane Temple,
who died 1914. Both buried at Bramans Corners, New York.

73 ELIZABETH AMANDA LIDDLE, born September 8, 1847;
died September 28, 1850.

74 IDA ANN LIDDLE, born December 15, 1850; died February
26, 1880. Married September 11, 1872, to Alonzo Van
Patten. Children 152-154.

75 MARY ARABELLE LIDDLE, born June 19, 1855. Married
January 15, 1890, to John E. Cullings, who died May 7,
1903. Residence, Duanesburg, New York.

Children of William Liddle (21) and Delia Fuller:

76 WILLIAM JAMES LIDDLE, born 1845; died March 13, 1872.
Married Harriet Edwards who was born November 6,
1847. Residence, Schenectady, New York. Child 155.

77 WARREN FULLER LIDDLE, born November 3, 1849; died
August 30, 1918. Married Martha J. Becker, born August
26, 1849; died October 16, 1891. Married again Isa Becker,
born July 25, 1856. Residence, Cobbelskill, New York.

Children of James Liddle (22) and Maria Vanderpool:

77A MARY GIFFORD LIDDLE, born March 13, 1854. Married
June 14, 1888, to Delmot Gregg.

77B ABRAM LIDDLE, married Leah Belle Cullings. Children
155A-155C.

Children of Mary Liddle (23) and Alexander D. Jones:

78 DELOS JONES, born November 9, 1848; died June 8, 1909.
Married Margaret I. Snell June 18, 1878. Married again
December, 1888 to Carrie Tanner. Children 156-159.

79 MARY ANN JONES, born July, 1850; died young.

80 BEATTA JONES, born December 9, 1851.

81 MARY ELIZABETH JONES, born April 4, 1856. Married
Charles Avery, March 7, 1877. Children 160-163.

82 NANCY JONES, born August 18, 1855.

83 ALEXANDER LIDDLE JONES, born October 30, 1860. Married
Dora L. Mosher, April 2, 1890. Child 164.

Children of Robert Duncan Liddle (25) and Abigail Liddle (43) daughter of (16):

84 JOHN SIDNEY LIDDLE, born October 1, 1850. Married March 24, 1844 to Mary Turlock. Residence, Gilbert, Iowa. Children 165-167.

85 SARAH SMITH LIDDLE, born July 15, 1853; died May 18, 1875.

86 NANCY LIDDLE, born March 1, 1855. Married December 24, 1874, to Silas Van Patten. Children 168-172.

87 ROBERT JAMES LIDDLE, born December 5, 1856. Married December 20, 1881, to Belle McMillan. Children 173-176.

Children of William Liddle (26) and Mary Liddle (44) daughter of (16):

88 FRANCIS W. LIDDLE, born April 16, 1857; died June 28, 1897, at Cedar Rapids, Iowa. Born at Gilbert, Iowa. Married Clara Spring, May 9, 1886. Children 177-178.

89 WILLIAM E. LIDDLE, born June 6, 1858; died April 3, 1859.

90 MARGARET B. LIDDLE, born December 22, 1860. Married William V. Wilson, October 21, 1880. He died June 14, 1914. Children 179-180.

91 JOHN A. LIDDLE, born July 6, 1863; died Schenectady, New York.

92 ALBERTUS S. LIDDLE, born March 29, 1865; died August 27, 1887, at Long Pine, Nebraska. Buried at Gilbert, Iowa. Unmarried.

93 JAMES E. LIDDLE, born May 7, 1867; died November 15, 1894, at Preston, Iowa. Buried at Gilbert, Iowa.

94 MARYELIZABETH LIDDLE, born July, 1869. Married August 18, 1884, at Ames, Iowa, to Adello H. Seaver. Children 181-184.

95 ROBERT WYLEY LIDDLE, born October 28, 1871. Married September 8, 1909, at Raymond, South Dakota, to Lizzie Adair.

96 JANET ELLA LIDDLE, born October 21, 1873. Married July 3, 1896, to Orace F. Spring of Preston, Iowa. Children 185-186.

Fourth Generation
Robert Liddle Branch

Children of Mary Elizabeth Liddle (29) and John Fletcher Ernest:

97 RICHARD SCHUYLER ERNEST, Married Etta Gordon. Children 187-188.

98 ALFRED COOKMAN ERNEST, Married Fanny Schuyler. Children 189-191.

99 WILLIAM E. ERNEST, Married Lena Ruff. Children 192-193.

100 HARRY LIDDLE ERNEST, Married Antoinette Van Horn.

Child of Jeanette R. (Liddle) and George Serviss:

101 ALEXANDER LIDDLE SERVISS, married Elizabeth Mehlman.

Child of Ida Marie Liddle (34) and Harry Sherbourn:

102 JOHN SHERBOURN, married Pearl Budd Shafer.

Child of Henry R. Wright (38) and Emma Morgan:

103 ALICE MORGAN WRIGHT, Artist. State Secretary of Suffrage. Residence, Albany, New York.

Children of Alexander Liddle (42) and Barbary Gregg:

104 ROBERT A. LIDDLE, born December 4, 1856. Married February 6, 1884, to Rebecca Wemple, born July 13, 1862. Children 194-196.

105 ANDREW G. LIDDLE, born February 23, 1859. Married Lillie De Fourt who was born January 16, 1864. Children 197-199.

Child of Alexander Liddle (42) and Margaret (Crowell) Passage:

106 JEANETTE LIDDLE, born March 17, 1878. Married June 24, 1908, to Russell Motte who was born November 13, 1874. Children 200-202.

Children of Ann Elizabeth Liddle (45) and George McFarlan:

107 EVA XELIA MCFARLAN, born August 7, 1857; died September 13, 1860.

108 CHARLES LIDDLE MCFARLAN, born October 17, 1855.
Married Margaret Whitbeck, March 7, 1885.

109 MARGARET LENA MCFARLAN, born August 25, 1861.
Married August 16, 1884, to William E. Emery.

110 JENNIE LYLE MCFARLAN, born December 27, 1862; died
January 10, 1864.

111 ABBIE ANN MCFARLAN, born January 17, 1864. Married
July 12, 1884, to Albert M. Bissell, who was born May 23,
1858, at Macomb, Illinois. Children 203-211.

112 SARAH JANE MCFARLAN, born July 8, 1866. Married
November 17, 1889, to William Roth.

113 BESSIE GIBBARD MCFARLAN, born September 14, 1867.
Married March 17, 1887, to Charles E. Spencer. Children
211A-211C.

114 MARY GIFFORD MCFARLAN, born January 5, 1869.
Married March 25, 1891, to Charles H. Davidson.

115 BARBARY LIDDLE MCFARLAN, born April 23, 1870.
Married November 9, 1894, to Preston L. Gay. Child
211D.

116 ADDIE BELLE MCFARLAN, born July 10, 1871. Married
February 18, 1890, to James W. Clemens at Boone, Iowa,
by the Reverend Lamb. Child 212. Married again April
2, 1895, to Samuel J. Starr at Tama City, Iowa. Children
213-214.

117 KATE VEDDER MCFARLAN, born October 31, 1872. Died
October 23, 1879.

118 MARTHA RAMSEY MCFARLAN, born November 18, 1874.
Married October 22, 1894 to William E. Hanson.

Children of Charles Liddle (46) and Abigail White. Children
all born in Duanesburg, New York:

119 ARTHUR LIDDLE, born June 10, 1865; died June 8, 1867.

120 FRANCES MARY LIDDLE, born March 4, 1867. Married
October 13, 1886, to George Lobdell Fideler, who was
born December 23, 1864, at Watervliet, New York.
Residence, Delanson, New York. Children 215-217.

121 ROBERT LIDDLE, born October 1, 1886. Married August
29, 1901, to Clara M. Frisby, born December 16, 1875.
Residence, Bramans Corners. Children 218-220.

122 JACOB LIDDLE, born August 1, 1870. Married September 12, 1906, to Harriet Van Ness, born May 8, 1874; died April, 1911. Married again September 14, 1911, to Kate Bender, born March 11, 1881, from Montgomery County, New York. Residence, Johnstown, New York. Child 221.

123 JEANETTE LIDDLE, born December 4, 1871. Married August 19, 1902, to L. Lee Terpaning, born January 7, 1873. Residence, Summit, Schoharie County, New York. Children 221A-225.

124 AUGUSTA LIDDLE, born August 26, 1875. Married February 16, 1898, to Fredrick Albert Sears, born May 2, 1868, at Saratoga, New York. Children 226-227.

125 MAHALA LIDDLE, born May 17, 1878. Married May 9, 1900, to Edgar Seldon Brown.

Children of Thomas Gifford Liddle (47) and Mary Jane McFarlan:

126 MARY BELLE LIDDLE, born October 24, 1866. Married at Boone, Iowa, May 31, 1898, to William Lincoln Troyes, who was born at Anawan, Henry County, Illinois, February 9, 1863. Residence, Etiwanda, California. Children 228-229.

127 JENNIE B. LIDDLE, born December 5, 1876. Died December 23, 1897.

128 ROBERT G. LIDDLE, born August 9, 1877. Married June 21, 1903, at Watertown, Wisconsin, to Inez Brown. Children 230-233.

Children of Robert William Liddle (49) and Adalaid Dix. Children all born in New Fane, New York:

128A ERNEST WILLIAM LIDDLE, born April 15, 1870. Married Edith Dunn, December 21, 1893, at Gilbert Station, Iowa. They adopted a child Adalaid, April, 1915.

128B ABRAM DIX LIDDLE, born October 29, 1874. Married January 1, 1907, to Myrtle A. Mayturn of Des Moines, Iowa. Child 233A.

128C ELLEN DIANTHIA LIDDLE, born May 7, 1877. Married at Gilbert, Iowa, June 6, 1900, to Reverend Anthony G. Beechman.

128D ROBERT ALEXANDER LIDDLE, born October 25, 1888. Married December 25, 1912, to Francys Carpenter at Des Moines, Iowa.

Children of Angus McDermit Liddle (50) and Ann Elizabeth Smith:

129 HENRY RAYMOND LIDDLE, born August 10, 1884. Married February 20, 1912, to Violetta E. Planck, born June 13, 1879. Child 234.

130 ANNA MABEL LIDDLE, born July 12, 1889; died June 11, 1913.

131 CLARENCE ROMEYN LIDDLE, born August 15, 1893.

Children of Robert James Liddle (55) and Jane Dunning:

132 NETTIE LIDDLE.

133 WILLIAM LIDDLE.

134 CLARENCE LIDDLE.

135 LINA MAY LIDDLE.

136 HELEN LIDDLE.

Children of Leah Jeanette Liddle (56) and John Ingersoll:

137 NETTIE INGERSOLL, born August 28, 1862. Married December 10, 1885, to Nelson D. Vedder, born March 21, 1862; died December 4, 1891. Residence, Fultonville, New York. Children 235-237.

138 ALEXANDER INGERSOLL, born June 1, 1864. Married October 22, 1902, to Emma S. Francisco. Children 238-241.

139 JOHN L. INGERSOLL, born August 29, 1866.

140 SARAH KATHERN INGERSOLL, born July 18, 1869. Married July 20, 1870, to William J. Avery. Children 242-243.

Child of Elizabeth Amelia Liddle (60) and William J. McClure:

141 GRACE McCLURE, born May 17, 1883. Married December 16, 1908, to Ordell Avery, born August 9, 1884. Children 244-245.

Children of Andrew Thomas McMillan (63) and Cathern Elizabeth McMillan:

141A FRANK McMILLAN, born March 9, 1868. Married Marion Darron.

141B FLORENCE McMILLAN, born March 24, 1871. Married
William James McMillan. Child 245A.

141C MARY McMILLAN, born April 24, 1873. Married October
17, 1894, to Albert J. Moore. Child 245B.

141D SAMUEL McMILLAN, born January 25, 1875.

Child of Benjamin McMillan (67) and Elizabeth Stillwell:

141E ANNA B. McMILLAN, born January 20, 1873.
Twin children of second wife, Mary L. Stillwell:

141F JOHN D. McMILLAN, born September 16, 1888. Married
Lucy Waldern.

141G JESSIE B. McMILLAN, born September 16, 1888.

Children of George Thomas Liddle (71) and Lydia Vanderpool:

142 FRANK LIDDLE, born August 5, 1866; died February 25,
1867.

143 CARRIE V. LIDDLE, born August 21, 1868. Married April
30, 1889, to Arthur Cullings. Residence, Schenectady,
New York. Child 246.

144 CATHERN MARANDA LIDDLE, born May 16, 1871; died
January 2, 1872.

145 MARY BELLE LIDDLE, born March 12, 1874; died April
19, 1875.

146 ELLA JANE LIDDLE, born April 16, 1876. Married October
25, 1899, to Eugene Wood. Residence, Schenectady, New
York.

Children of William Henry Liddle (72) and Zelphina Jane Knapp:

147 CORA BELLE LIDDLE, born August 27, 1869. Married
July 2, 1889, to Delos Chisholm. Child 247.

148 GEORGE WILLIAM LIDDLE, born October 15, 1871.
Married January 31, 1894, to Harriet Tiffany. Resided
1905 in Esperence, New York. (See Descendants of
Thomas Durfee, Vol. II, by Wm. F. Reed, for her lineage.)

149 JOHN MILTON LIDDLE, born May 23, 1876. Married March
27, 1902, to Bessie M. Hutchinson. Children 248-250.

150 CHARLES HENRY LIDDLE, born May, 1879. Married in
1905 to Ella Snell. Residence, Schenectady, New York.
Children 251-252.

151 MARY ETHEL LIDDLE, born January 1896. Married June, 1914, to Augustus J. Crouse. Residence, Schenectady, New York. Child 253.

Children of Ida Ann Liddle (74) and Alonzo Van Patten:

152 WILLIAM HENRY VAN PATTEN, born April, 1874; died 1890.
153 JUSTUS WRIGHT VAN PATTEN, born August 21, 1876; died February 4, 1897.
154 IRVEN ROY VAN PATTEN, born June 1879. Married Ida Belle Van Patten in November, 1902. Children 254-255.

Child of William James Liddle (76) and Harriet E. Edwards of Schenectady, New York:

155 HENRY S. LIDDLE, born October 28, 1871. Married Anna Hillabrant, born July 13, 1872. Residence, Piseco, New York. Occupation, physician. Child 256.

Children of Abram Liddle (77B) and Leah Belle Cullings:

155A CLARA LIDDLE.
155B EDNA LIDDLE.
155C BERTHA LIDDLE.

Children of Delos Jones (78) and Margaret Snell:

156 WALTER JONES, born October, 1884; died July, 1885.
157 IDA SNELL JONES, born June, 1886. Married November 15, 1909, to Joseph A. Hines. Children 257-258.

Children of second wife, Carrie Tanner:

158 AMANDA TANNER JONES, born September 9, 1893.
159 MARY L. JONES, born October 15, 1897.

Children of Mary Elizabeth Jones (81) and Charles Avery:

160 EVA AVERY, born July 13, 1881.
161 MARY LIDDLE AVERY, born June 22, 1884. Married June 5, 1906, to William M. Fergurson.
162 ALICE AVERY, born October 28, 1885. Married October 28, 1915, to Ben Walter Jones.
163 HARLEH EUGENE AVERY, born November 16, 1900.

Child of Alexander Liddle Jones (83) and Dora L. Mosher:

164 HARRY AMOS JONES, born November 6, 1892.

Children of John Sidney Liddle (84) and Mary Turlock:
165 LUELLA LIDDLE.
166 ABBIE LIDDLE. Died.
167 ZENIA LIDDLE.

Children of Nancy Liddle (86) and Silas Van Patten:
168 IDA BELLE LIDDLE VAN PATTEN.
169 SARAH SMITH VAN PATTEN.
170 ARTHUR VAN PATTEN.
171 HOWARD VAN PATTEN.
172 FREMONT VAN PATTEN.

Children of Robert James Liddle (87) and Belle McMillan:
173 JANE LIDDLE.
174 RALPH LIDDLE.
175 EARL LIDDLE.
176 BERTHA LIDDLE.

Children of Francis W. Liddle (88) and Clara Spring:
177 HAZEL K. LIDDLE, born September 1, 1889.
178 CHESTER L. LIDDLE, born January 31, 1896.

Children of Margaret B. Liddle (90) and William V. Wilson.
Children born at Gilbert, Iowa:
179 INFANT DAUGHTER, born and died April 13, 1882.
180 CLARA BELLE WILSON, born September 5, 1886.
Married at Gilbert, Iowa, March 26, 1897, to James
Rosco Dodds. Children 259-261.

Children of Mary Elizabeth Liddle (94) and Adello H. Seaver.
Children born at Maquoketa, Iowa:
181 VIVIAN M. SEAVER, born March 23, 1896.
182 GERTRUDE SEAVER, born July 1, 1897.
183 RUTH SEAVER, born October 7, 1901.
184 LEONARD WILLIAM SEAVER, born November 23, 1910.

Children of Janet Ella Liddle (96) and Orace F. Spring:
185 SEYMOUR O. SPRING, born August 6, 1899, at North
Yakima, Washington.
186 GLADYS LIDDLE SPRING, born March 7, 1914, at North
Yakima, Washington.

Fifth Generation
Robert Liddle Branch

Children of Richard Scuyler Ernest (97) and Etta Gordon:
187 MARION ERNEST.
188 GORDON ERNEST.

Children of Alfred Cookman Ernest (98) and Fanny Schuyler:
189 ALBERT SCHUYLER ERNEST.
190 JOHN FLETCHER ERNEST.
191 GEORGE SCHUYLER ERNEST.

Children of William G. Ernest (99) and Lena Ruff:
192 HELEN M. ERNEST.
193 ROBERT ERNEST.

Children of Robert A. Liddle (104) and Rebecca Wemple:
194 JAMES W. LIDDLE, born October 14, 1885.
195 BARBARY G. LIDDLE, born August 2, 1887. Married October 21, 1908, to Barton Scace, born January 7, 1887. Children 262-263.
196 ANNA C. LIDDLE, born October 16, 1897. Married November, 1913, to George Wagner, born January 26, 1888. Residence, Duanesburg, New York. Child 264.

Children of Andrew G. Liddle (105) and Lillie De Fourt:
197 ALEXANDER LIDDLE, born July 7, 1883. Married Elizabeth Quick. Children 265-266.
198 EDITH LIDDLE, born January 26, 1886. Married January 10, 1906 to Grover Darrow.
199 LAURA LIDDLE, born May 6, 1890. Married Andrew G. Quick. Residence, Duanesburg, New York. Child 267.

Children of Jeanette Liddle (106) and Russell C. Motte:
200 MARGARET CROWELL MOTTE, born June 21, 1909.
201 MERVIN STUART MOTTE, born July 25, 1910.
202 RAYMOND RUSSELL MOTTE, born March 26, 1913.

Children of Abbie Ann McFarlan (111) and Albert M. Bissell. Residence, Foley, Minnesota:

203 RUTH BISSELL, born September 10, 1885, at Edmunds, North Dakota. Married February 6, 1907, to Robert H. Bradshaw.

204 WALTER W. BISSELL, born August 15, 1887, at Gilbert, Iowa. Married July 29, 1901, to Goldie Snyder, born December 27, 1896. Children 268-270.

205 BLAIR BISSELL, born June 24, 1889, at Gilbert, Iowa; died May 1, 1907, at Seattle, Washington.

206 GEORGE A. BISSELL, born April 26, 1891, at Gilbert, Iowa.

207 FAITH BISSELL, born December 21, 1893, at Humboldt, Iowa.

208 PAUL P. BISSELL, born June 10, 1896.

209 JOHN P. BISSELL, born November 22, 1897.

210 ROBERT LIDDLE BISSELL, born January 11, 1899.

211 ELSIE LOUISA BISSELL, born February 25, 1900.

Children of Bessie Gibbard McFarlan (113) and Charles Edward Spencer:

211A VERA ELIZABETH SPENCER, born November 11, 1889. Married January 9, 1911, to Ulyssis D. Wood, born 1885. Children 270A-270B.

211B JAMES WALLACE SPENCER, born October 16, 1894. Married February 13, 1917, to Lucia May Tillon, born September 1897. Child 270C.

211C CHARLES CRAWFORD SPENCER, born January 13, 1897. Married April 26, 1918, to Josephine Sutton, born January 19, 1900.

Child of Barbary Liddle McFarlan (115) and Preston Lee Gay:

211D CONKLIN GEORGE GAY, born April 6, 1896.

Child of Addie Bell McFarlan (116) and James W. Clemens:

212 CHARLES SPURGEN CLEMENS, born July 12, 1891. Later had his name changed to McFarlan to retain the family name.

Children by second marriage to Samuel J. Starr:

213 NEAL DOW STARR, born July 2, 1897.

214 CLARA BARTON STARR, born December 21, 1900. Residence, 1555 East 61st Street, Chicago, Illinois.

Children of Frances Mary Liddle (120) and George Lobdell Fideler:

215 JOHN WARD FIDELER, born February 16, 1890.
216 CHARLES MYRON FIDELER, born September 28, 1894.
217 NATHAN HALE FIDELER, born October 11, 1901.
Children all born at Duanesburg, New York.

Children of Robert Liddle (121) and Clara M. Frisby:

218 CHARLES HENRY LIDDLE, born September 21, 1902.
219 HELEN A. LIDDLE, born February 12, 1906.
220 WARREN MILTON LIDDLE, born January 14, 1908.

Child of Jacob Liddle (122) and Harriet Van Ness:

221 FREDRICK LIDDLE, born October 26, 1908. Residence, Johnstown, New York.

Children of Jeanette Liddle (123) and Landlan Lee Terpaning:

221A HAROLD L. TERPANING, born May 2, 1903; died August 27, 1903.
222 ALMA TERPANING, born September 20, 1904.
223 LUCY LEE TERPANING, born April 6, 1906.
224 MARY JANE TERPANING, born September 11, 1907.
225 MAX TERPANING, born March 1, 1911. Residence, Delanson, New York.

Children of Augusta Liddle (124) and Fredrick Albert Sears:

226 WILLIAM CARLTON SEARS, born September 4, 1899; died July 23, 1913.
227 FLORENCE MAY SEARS, born February 5, 1914.

Children of Mary Belle Liddle (126) and William Lincoln Troyes. Residence, Etiwanda, California:

228 BESSIE I. TROYES, born February 22, 1903.
229 PAUL D. TROYES, born January 5, 1910.

Children of Robert G. Liddle (128) and Inez Brown:

230 DEWITT LIDDLE, born August 16, 1907.
231 ISABELLE LIDDLE, born November 26, 1910.
232 INEZ LIDDLE } Twins, born August 31, 1913.
233 ROBERTA LIDDLE } Residence, Etiwanda, California.

Child of Abram Dix Liddle (128B) and Myrtle A. Mayturn:

233A LOUISA MAYTURN LIDDLE, born February 2, 1911.

Children of Ellen Dianthia Liddle (128C) and Reverend Anthony G. Beechman:

234 FLORENCE A. BEECHMAN, born 1901.

234A KATHERYN BEECHMAN, born 1910.

Child of Robert A. Liddle (131A) and Francys Carpenter:

234B WILLIAM E. LIDDLE, born March 5, 1914.

Child of Henry Raymond Liddle (129) and Violetta E. Plauck:

234C BEVERLY RAYMOND LIDDLE, born February 9, 1916.

Children of Nettie Ingersoll (137) and Nelson D. Vedder:

235 LELAND NELSON VEDDER, born December 24, 1886. Married March 24, 1917, to Grace Irving Quackinbush.

236 EARL INGERSOLL VEDDER, born October 12, 1888. Married March 15, 1912, to Josephine Elizabeth Christian.

237 ZERAH VEDDER, born October 3, 1890. Married June 28, 1916, to Edith Hansen.

Children of Alexander Ingersoll (138) and Emma Francisco:

238 JOHN ABBOT INGERSOLL, born March 6, 1903.

239 GEORGE ALEXANDER INGERSOLL, born March 26, 1906.

240 EDWARD LIDDLE INGERSOLL, born November 15, 1907.

241 SARAH JANETTE INGERSOLL, born January 23, 1909.

Children of Sarah Kathern Ingersoll (140) and William J. Avery:

242 HETTY LIDDLE AVERY, born May 25, 1874. Married Wesley McDugal, December 25, 1894. He was born February 27, 1864. Child 271.

243 JESSIE B. AVERY, born March 11, 1878. Married October 26, 1898, to Cora Belle McDugal. She was born October 28, 1878. Child 272.

Children of Grace McClure (141) and Ordell Avery:

244 WINIFRED ELOISE AVERY, born February 5, 1914.

245 MARY ELIZABETH AVERY, born October 13, 1916.

Child of Florence McMillan (141B) and William James McMillan:

245A MARY JANE MCMILLAN.

Child of Mary McMillan (141C) and Albert J. Moore:

245B IRENE MOORE, born April 10, 1907.

Child of Carrie V. Liddle (143) and Arthur Cullings:

246 CORA ETHEL CULLINGS, born January, 1898. Residence, Wabash Avenue No. 22, Schenectady, New York.

Child of Cora Belle Liddle (147) and Delos Chisholm:

247 CAROLINE MAE CHISHOLM, married November 9, 1911, to Harold William Rodgers. Residence, Schenectady, New York.

Children of John Milton Liddle (149) and Bessie M. Hutchins:

248 JESSIE ALICE LIDDLE, born December 27, 1902.
249 MYRTLE MARY LIDDLE, born September 30, 1906.
250 EILENE HUTCHINS LIDDLE, born March 26, 1914. Residence, Windsor, Vermont.

Children of Charles Henry Liddle (150) and Ella Snell.

251 MARY ELIZABETH LIDDLE, born December 13, 1907.
252 KENNETH LIDDLE, born June 20, 1909. Residence, Schenectady, New York.

Child of Mary Ethel Liddle (151) and Augustus Crouse:

253 GEORGE WILLIAM CROUSE, born July 22, 1916. Residence, Schenectady, New York.

Children of Irven Roy Van Patten (154) and Ida Belle Van Patten:

254 DOROTHY HELEN VAN PATTEN, born August, 1903.
255 IDA VIRGINIA VAN PATTEN, born November, 1907.

Child of Dr. Henry S. Liddle (155) and Anna Hillabrant:

256 SANFORD E. LIDDLE, born March 11, 1904.

Children of Ida Snell Jones (157) and Joseph A. Hines:

257 DORIS A. HINES, born December 4, 1910.
258 CHARLES DELOS HINES, born December 23, 1912; died September, 1914.

Children of Clara Belle Wilson (180) and James Rosco Dodds. Children born at Maquoketa:

259 EDWARD E. DODDS, born March 19, 1909.
260 VEDA IRENE DODDS, born June 18, 1911.
261 ROBERT WILLIAM DODDS, born November 11, 1915.

Sixth Generation
Robert Liddle Branch

Children of Barbary Liddle (195) and Barton Scace:
262 ROBERT W. SCACE, born December 26, 1909.
263 RAYMOND L. SCACE, born June 16, 1915.

Child of Anna C. Liddle (196) and George Wagner:
264 PAULINE E. WAGNER, born June 10, 1916.

Children of Alexander Liddle (197) and Elizabeth Quick:
265 EVELINE LIDDLE, born September 8, 1914.
266 HELEN LIDDLE, born June 3, 1916.

Child of Laura Liddle (199) and Andrew G. Quick:
267 ANDREW G. QUICK, JR., born January 7, 1910.

Children of Walter M. Bissell (204) and Goldie Snyder:
268 MARION BISSELL, born February 16, 1913.
269 ALBERT BISSELL, JR., born December 19, 1914.
270 VIVIAN BISSELL, born June 28, 1916.

Children of Vera Elizabeth Spencer (211A) and Ulyssis Wood:
270A PERCY CLIFFORD WOOD, born July 29, 1912.
270B BESSIE JANE WOOD, born September 15, 1914.

Child of James Wallace Spencer (211B) and Lucia May Tillon:
270C ANNABELLE SPENCER, born September 9, 1918.

Child of Hetty Liddle (242) and Wesley McDugal:
271 RALPH WESLEY McDUGAL, born June 17, 1897.

Child of Jessie B. Avery (243) and Cora Belle McDugal:
272 ELSWORTH W. AVERY, born February 6, 1900.

First Generation
Adam Liddle Branch

ADAM LIDDLE (3) son of John Liddle and Elizabeth Everson (see John Liddle records). These records were not received until the John and Robert Liddle records had been compiled; therefore they are arranged separately. This Adam Liddle is the brother of John Liddle, Jr. (2).

Adam Liddle (3), born Fonda, New York, according to church records, April 2, 1785, baptized April 22, 1785 at Fonda, New York. A confliction in records exists as the family Bible records his birth April 22, 1785. Baptism performed by the Reverend Thomas Romeyn, Pastor of the Reformed Church of Fonda.

He married October 5, 1817, Melinda Myra Von Crapser (changed to Crapsey) who was born August 12, 1794. She died November 18, 1866. Adam Liddle died October 11, 1877. Both are buried at West Shelby, Orleans County, New York. He served in the War of 1812, as private in Captain Elnathan Cobb's Company, 147th Regiment (Woods), New York Militia. He enlisted October 27th, 1814, and was discharged November 16, 1814 at Smiths Mills. His residence was Manlius, Onondaga County, New York State. Children 4-11. See Von Crapsey records, page 34.

Second Generation
Adam Liddle Branch

Children of Adam Liddle (3) and wife, Melinda Myra Von Crapsey:

4 JOHN PERRY LIDDLE, born December 5, 1818; died August 15, 1821.

5 JACOB TOMPKINS LIDDLE, born in Onondaga County, New York, August 28, 1820; died in Slidell, Louisiana, March 10, 1905. Married to Hannah McNeil of Lockport, New York, by Reverend Mr. Perkins, October 12, 1846. She died in Slidell, Louisiana, November 17, 1904. She was born in Niagara County, New York, September 16, 1825. Children 12-17.

6 TRYPHOSA JEANETTE LIDDLE, born August 9, 1822; died November 18, 1852. Married December 31, 1846, to Harvey M. Handy. Children 18-19.

7 ADALINE MINERVA LIDDLE, born August 28, 1825; died October 20, 1906. Married January 10, 1853, to James S. Partridge. Children 20-21.

8 ADAM PERRY LIDDLE, born September 9, 1827. Married October 11, 1853, Eliza McBrerty, born February 6, 1834; died May 11, 1906. Adam died September 11, 1914. Both buried at Manton, Michigan. Children 22-23.

9 MOSES GRANDSON WASHINGTON LIDDLE, born November 17, 1829. No record.

10 ANNA ALZIRA LIDDLE, born March 20, 1833, at Shelby, Orleans County, New York. Married Peter P. Richtmyer February 6, 1853. He died June 18, 1909, at Jerome, Michigan. Children 24-27.

11 JOHN GRIFFITH CRAPSEY LIDDLE, born April 20, 1835; died September 12, 1875. Married May 14, 1862, Eliza A. Noble. Son Charles Ashley Liddle drowned in Bayon at Hansboro, Mississippi, February 1884.

Third Generation
Adam Liddle Branch

Children of Jacob Tompkins Liddle (5) and Hannah (McNeil) Liddle:

12 CHARLES McNEIL LIDDLE, born in Mississippi City, Mississippi, September 17, 1852. Married to Clara Bloomfield in Hansboro, Mississippi, June 6, 1876, by Reverend J. B. Hamberlin. Clara Bloomfield, his wife, born in New Orleans, Louisiana, September 29, 1853. Children 28-32.

13 FRANK J. LIDDLE, born in Hansboro, Mississippi, May 28, 1855; died in Hansboro, October 10, 1858.

14 MARY EFFIE LIDDLE, born in Pass Christian, Mississippi, April 23, 1857. Married Charles E. Everett in Hansboro, Mississippi, February 11, 1877 by Reverend J. B. Hamberlin. C. E. Everett died February 25, 1902. Children 33-36.

15 HELEN EMMA LIDDLE, born in Hansboro, Mississippi, November 18, 1860. Married first a Mr. Lyon. Married again in Hansboro, Mississippi, to Homer E. Flournoy, February 11, 1880, by the Reverend Dr. S. H. Ford of St. Louis, Missouri. They reside in Aliceville, Alabama. Homer E. Flournoy was born at Linnaeus, Missouri, August 27, 1851. His father was Gibson Flournoy, a captain in the Mexican and Civil wars, born near Richmond, Virginia, January 24, 1812, and died at Meridian Mississippi, November 1892. Mr. Homer Flournoy's uncle, A. W. Flournoy was elected speaker of the legislature of Missouri for a number of years, after which he moved to Boise City, Idaho, where he was elected judge of the county and district courts. Children of Homer. 37-42.

16 ELLA ROSA BELL LIDDLE, born in Hansboro, Mississippi, January 23, 1862. Married to Fritz Salmen in Hansboro, Mississippi, November 23, 1882, by Reverend Oscar D. Bowen. Children 43-45.

17 WILLIAM ROBERT LEE LIDDLE, born in Hansboro, Miss-

issippi, November 3, 1864; died in Hansboro, Mississippi, October 12, 1895.

Children of Tryphosa Jeanette Liddle (6) and Harvey M. Handy:

18 MINERVA HANDY, married Albert Wilcox. No further record.
19 HARVEY DOWNEY HANDY, residence, Texas. No further record.

Children of Adaline Minerva Liddle (7) and James S. Partridge:

20 ALLIE (ALZIRA) C. PARTRIDGE.
21 ROSELLA J. PARTRIDGE, married Rockwell.

Children of Adam Perry Liddle (8) and Eliza McBrerty:

22 PERRY EUGENE LIDDLE, born February 8, 1856. Married Vinnie Stoner July 4, 1882, by Reverend Bascom at Manton, Michigan. Residence, Battle Creek, Michigan. Children 46-48.
23 JOHN GRANT LIDDLE, born November 14, 1868. Married Hattie Lewella Baker January 13, 1895 by Reverend Chapman at Pleasant Lake, Michigan. Residence, Buckley, Michigan. Children 49-52.

Children of Anna Alzira (Liddle) (10) Richtmyer, and Peter P. Richtmyer:

24 ESTELLA MARIA RICHTMYER, born February 8, 1854. Married John B. Alley February 8, 1872 by Reverend S. Fowler of Hillsdale, Michigan.
25 RODELLA A. RICHTMYER, born August 8, 1857; died April 28, 1915. Married February 19, 1882, Thomas Worden Tryon, by Reverend Branch Somerset. Children 53-54.
26 SARAH ADDIE RICHTMYER, born May 7, 1859. Married Stanley C. Murrey by Reverend Huntsberger November 8, 1882. Child 54A.
27 EVA ELIZA RICHTMYER, born April 20, 1861. Married Gustare Francois Phillip Pothin in Orange Park, Florida, June 3, 1891. He was born in France at Chalon Sur Marne Department Marne et Saone (Junction Marne and Saone Rivers). Married again her brother-in-law, Thomas Worden Tryon.

Fourth Generation
Adam Liddle Branch

Children of Charles McNeil Liddle (12) and Clara (Bloomfield) Liddle:

28 ARTHUR BLOOMFIELD LIDDLE, born in Hansboro, Mississippi, October 27, 1877.

29 JACOB T. LIDDLE, JR., born in Hansboro, Mississippi, November 14, 1880. Married Effie Hall May 29, 1900. Residence, Slidell, Louisiana. Children 55-57.

30 HORACE BLOOMFIELD LIDDLE, born in Hansboro, Mississippi, November 9, 1886. Married Mrs. Emily Decker O'Brien October 12, 1916, by Reverend Spurgeon Wingo. Residence, Slidell, Louisiana.

31 EDWARD BLOOMFIELD LIDDLE, born Hansboro, Mississippi, April 20, 1888. Married Louisa Mix at Jackson, Mississippi, June 10, 1915. Residence, Colorado Springs, Colorado. Physician.

32 GLADYS BLOOMFIELD LIDDLE, born Hansboro, Mississippi, November 3, 1890. Married Dr. John Armstrong Watkins in Slidell, Louisiana, November 8, 1911 by Reverend Oscar D. Bowen. Residence, Cincinnati, Ohio. Children 58-59.

Children of Mary Effie Liddle (14) and Charles E. Everett:

33 CHARLES A. EVERETT, born October 16, 1879 at Hansboro, Mississippi. Married in New Orleans, Louisiana, January 8, 1906 to Miss Alice Carr, by Reverend Beverly Warner. She was born in New Orleans, Louisiana, November 5, 1885. Child 60.

34 ELERE EVERETT, born Hansboro, Mississippi, February 21, 1887. Married Norman Gillis in Slidell, Louisiana, December 27, 1906, by Reverend Oscar D. Bowen. Norman Gillis died in Covington, Louisiana, August 18, 1916. Children 61-63.

35 GEORGE WILLIAM EVERETT, born in Hansboro, Mississippi, June 25, 1885. Married Alice Welsh March 4, 1903, by

Judge John Y. Crow. Residence, Slidell, Louisiana. Children 64-66.

36 DONA LIDDLE EVERETT, born in Hansboro, Mississippi, September 12, 1891. Married to L. V. Cooley, Jr., in Slidell, Louisiana, by Reverend Oscar D. Bowen, May 22, 1913. Residence, Slidell, Louisiana. Children 67-68.

Children of Helen Emma (Liddle) (15) Flournoy and Homer E. Flournoy: Their children were all born in Meridian, Mississippi.

37 BERTIE ROSA FLOURNOY, born February 22, 1884. Married at Meridian, Mississippi, June 6, 1905, by Reverend Dr. T. J. Shipman, a Baptist Pastor, to James B. Hill of Mobile, Alabama, a sales manager for a wholesale hardware corporation in Birmingham, Alabama. Residence, Birmingham, Alabama.

38 HOMER EDWARD FLOURNOY, JR., born April 16, 1886. Married at San Antonio, Texas, June, 1907, to Ethel Elliott (formerly of Meridian, Mississippi) at her father's residence.

39 LILLIAN FLOURNOY, born May 16, 1887. Another record gives her birth May 15, 1888. Married by Reverend Dr. T. J. Shipman, December 24, 1908, to Joseph H. Baker, formerly of Lewisburg, N. C. He was born October 6, 1881, near Wakefield, N. C. Children 69-74.

40 JACOB T. FLOURNOY, born September 21, 1890.

41 EMMA FLOURNOY, born November 21, 1895. Residence, Aliceville, Alabama.

42 MARIE FLOURNOY, born October 23, 1898. Residence, Aliceville, Alabama.

Children of Ella Rosa Bell Liddle (16) and Fritz Salmen: These children were all born in Slidell, Louisiana.

43 ELAROSE LIDDLE SALMEN, born in Slidell, Louisiana, May 10, 1885. Married January 27, 1922 to William Henry Sullivan at Slidell, Louisiana.

44 FREDERICK WILLIAM SALMEN, born in Slidell, Louisiana, January 11, 1887.

45 LEE LIDDLE SALMEN, born in Slidell, Louisiana, March 3, 1890; died in Slidell, Louisiana, October 7, 1894.

Children of Perry Eugene Liddle (22) and Vinnie Stoner:

46 OLIVE MAY LIDDLE, born October 13, 1884.
47 CARL LIDDLE, born September 9, 1885.
48 ELIZABETH LIDDLE, born August 23, 1887. Married Frank Parker.
   Olive May and Carl reside in Battle Creek, Michigan.

Children of John Grant Liddle (23) and wife Hattie L. (Baker) Liddle:

49 FLORENCE LIDDLE, born May 22, 1897.
50 MILDRED LIDDLE, born March 26, 1899.
51 HOWARD LIDDLE, born April 13, 1901.
52 RALPH LIDDLE, born August 23, 1903. Residence, Buckley, Michigan.

Children of Rodella A. (Richtmyer) Tryon (25) and Thomas Worden Tryon:

53 CHARLES AUBREY TRYON, born February 25, 1888. Married August 4, 1910 at Tecumseh, Michigan, by Reverend Howard Moore, Bertha Ella Clark.
54 RETTA MARGERY TRYON, born March 15, 1892. Residence, Jerome, Michigan.

Child of Sarah Addie (Richtmyer) (26) and Stanley C. Murrey:

54A CLARENCE DALE MURREY, born in Moscow, Michigan, July 5, 1886. Married March 27, 1913 to Mrs. Martha Augusta (Haska) Bolsom. She was born in Cleveland, Ohio, August 6, 1886. Mrs. Bolsom had two children by her former husband, which Mr. Murrey adopted April 4, 1913. They have two children born to them. Children 75-78.

Fifth Generation
Adam Liddle Branch

Children of Jacob T. Liddle (29) and Effie (Hall) Liddle:
   Their children were all born in Slidell, Louisiana.
55 LYLA ODETTE LIDDLE, born May 26, 1901.
56 CHARLES M. LIDDLE, JR., born October 29, 1903.
57 J. T. LIDDLE, 3rd, born May 21, 1906.

Children of Gladys (Bloomfield Liddle) Watkins (32) and Dr. John A. Watkins of Cincinnati, Ohio:

58   GLADYS LIDDLE WATKINS, born September 18, 1914.
59   GERTRUDE ARMSTRONG WATKINS, born November 6, 1916.
These children were born in Pittsburg, Pennsylvania.

Child of Charles A. Everett (33) and Alice (Carr) Everett:
60   JANICE EVERETT, born in Slidell, Louisiana, Sept. 8, 1906.

Children of Elcre (Everett) Gillis (34) and Norman Gillis:
61   MARY ELIZABETH GILLIS, born January 9, 1908.
62   NORMAN EVERETT GILLIS, born January 2, 1910.
63   DAVID WILEY GILLIS, born April 24, 1912.
These children were born in Slidell, Louisiana.

Children of George William Everett (35) and Alice (Welsh):
64   LE REE WELSH EVERETT, born March 12, 1907.
65   CHARLES EDWARD EVERETT, born September 7, 1913.
66   GEORGE WILLIAM EVERETT, born December 30, 1919.
These children were born in Slidell, Louisiana.

Children of Dona (Liddle Everett) Cooley (36) and L. V. Cooley, Jr.:
67   LE VERRIER COOLEY, JR. 3rd, born March 2, 1916.
68   DAVID EVERETT COOLEY, born May 4, 1917.
These children were all born in Slidell, Louisiana.

Children of Lillian Flournoy (39) Baker and Joseph Baker:
69   JNO. LEWIS BAKER, born Thursday, February 3, 1910.
70   LILLIAN MATAROE BAKER, born Monday, January 1, 1912
71   EMMA JOSEPHINE BAKER, born Wednesday, Nov. 19, 1913.
72   JOE FLOURNOY BAKER, born Sunday, January 11, 1915.
73   CELESTIA LUCILE BAKER, born Sunday, May 6, 1917.
74   ETHEL MARIE BAKER, born Friday, December 12, 1919.
These children were born in Jackson, Mississippi.

Children of Clarence D. Murrey (54A) and Martha Augusta (Haska) (Bolsom) Murrey.
75   FRED BOLSOM MURREY.
76   FERN BOLSOM MURREY.
77   DALE STANLEY MURREY, born May 30, 1914.
78   DONALD CLARENCE MURREY, born June 10, 1920.

INDEX

John Liddle Branch

The John, Robert and Adam branches are each numbered separately beginning with "1." The number affixed to a name represents not a page number, but the genealogical number assigned to that person. Care should be exercised in referring to the John Liddle branch for names on this and the following page.

Abbey, Cora Luella, 136
Booth, Charlotte Amy, 157
Broadwell, Ernest Earl, 123A
"   Nellie Pearl, 125
"   Opal Agnes, 124
Carr, Arthur Tillman, 76
"   Carrie Louisa, 71
"   Charles F., 70
"   Clinton H., 73
"   Cora Eloise, 72
"   Freddie Liddle, 77
"   Gilbert H., 69
"   Minnie J., 74
"   Nellie Marie, 75
Engle, Marie Lorene, 134A
"   Russell George, 134B
Featherstone, Frances Leona, 175
"   Norman Fredene, 174
Fisk, Dorothy Aileen, 170
"   E. Juanita, 123
"   Holly Keyes, 122
"   Palmer K., 169
Gifford, Marjory Rose Morgan, 82A
"   Wendell P., 82
Hirst, Delelle E., 127
"   Halla Laveda, 130
"   James Vincent, 129
"   Martha Helene, 128
Kenyon, Edward H. Fay, 160
"   Jessie Oleta, 161
"   LeRoy Oakley, 158
"   Martha Arleen, 159
Keyes, Ely E., 63
"   Hazel Irene, 120
"   Ivan Gardner, 121
"   Kathern A., 62
"   Lillian J., 64
Liddle, Adam, 3
"   Alida May, 97
"   Alvina, 17
"   Bertha Helen, 91
"   Byron Jacob, 25
"   Caroline, 22
"   Cathern, 12
"   Cathern Marie, 24

Liddle, Charles Marcellus, 31
"   Clarence B., 142
"   Clayton, 96
"   David 3C-14
"   Earl Rowland, 141
"   Edna Aileen, 182
"   Eliza Eleanor, 9
"   Elizabeth, 21
"   Ernest Philo, 79
"   Esther, 93
"   Fannie, 18
"   Frank, 67
"   Frank Lyford, 98
"   Franklin, 55
"   Fred, 66
"   George, 56
"   Getty (Gertrude) Marie, 13
"   Gilbert, 6-33
"   Gilbert Van Deusen, 7
"   Gladys Eileen, 126
"   Harold, 92
"   Harriet, 26
"   Harriet Ann, 32
"   Harry, 90
"   Henry Mathew, 30
"   Henry Watson, 38
"   Herbert, 95
"   Hirum Gilbert, 19
"   Hugh, 2A
"   Inez Ruth, 140
"   Jacob, 3B-4
"   Jane, 16-58
"   Jannette, 1A
"   John 1-2-5-23-57
"   John Robert, 48
"   Julia Elizabeth, 34
"   Katherine Rebecca, 37
"   Kenneth, 94
"   Margaret, 3A
"   Marie Helen, 36
"   Martha D., 35
"   Mathew, 11
"   Melbourn Howard, 183
"   Morris, 40
"   Moses, 8

Liddle, Nancy, 4A-10
" Noyes, 41
" Oliver Longstreet, 135
" Orley Erwin, 78
" Philo, 20
" Ray, 65
" Roe, 68
" Sarah, 39
" Vance, 59
" William, 4B-15
" William Wellington, 27
Madaw, Wallace, 42
Mellen, Waive Lorane, 178
Miller, Carl, 151
" Charles Holly, 172
" Cyrel Claud, 149
" Edward D., 173
" Gardner, 152
" Hobart McKinley, 147
" Judson, 106
" Judson Nathan, 154
" Kenneth Karl, 150
" Mabel S., 104-153
" Marcia Belle McKinley, 148
" Miner, 105
" William F., 171
Moulton, Anna, 165
" Earl, 162
" Glen, 111
" Madelene May, 179
" Rexford, 164
" Walter, 163
McKinley, Bion Van Olinda, 99
" Byron, 47
" Caroline, 44
" Eugene Fritz, 101
" Florence Ida, 109
" Floy Olive, 102
" Fred Claud, 108
" Gilbert Liddle, 43
" Gilbert Ross, 143
" Hays Duncan, 45
" Jessie Pearl, 110
" John Hays, 155
" Marjorie Crouse, 145
" Mariette, 46

McKinley, Nellie Estelle, 107
" Reed, 144
" Richard Stephen, 156
" Uretta May, 100
" William, 146
Peterson, Arnold, 165A
Rhode, Jennie, 54
Schultz, Edward, 167
" Erma May, 166
Seeley, Florence Eugene, 138
" Floyd Noyes, 139
" Lucinda May, 137
Sides, Harold I., 89
" Raymond M., 88
Slocum, Harry D., 117
" Marion Jeanett, 168
Strail, James M., 103
Sweeder, Charles, 176
" Leo Vance, 177
Tanner, George Keyes, 119
" Gertrude E., 118
Trubey, Halla Belle, 80
" Valerie Anita, 81
Walker, Francis John, 133
" Joseph Henry, 134
" Martha May, 131B
" Robert Van Deusen, 132
" Valerie Elizabeth, 131A
" William Homer, 131
Welty, George Frank, 84
" Helen Frances, 85
" Harry Freese, 83
" Loren Austin, 87
" Russell, 86
Whitmore, Luella, 60
" Schuyler, 61
Young, Beula Ora, 115
" Cathern Borena, 114
" Emaline, 50
" Etta May Belle, 113
" Gilbert, 53
" Jacob Adelbert, 116
" Jacob Mathew, 51
" James K., 49
" Martha Maria, 52
" Wallace Franklin, 112

INDEX

Robert Liddle Branch

Avery, Alice, 162
" Eva, 160
" Harleh Eugene, 163
" Hetty Liddle, 242
" Jessie B., 243
" Mary Elizabeth, 245
" Mary Liddle, 161
" Winifred Eloise, 244
Beechman, Florence A., 234
" Katheryn, 234A
Bissell, Albert, 269
" Blair, 205
" Elsie Louisa, 211
" Faith, 207
" George A., 206
" John P., 209
" Marion, 268
" Paul, 208
" Ruth, 203
" Robert Liddle, 210
" Vivian, 270
" Walter W., 204
Chisholm, Caroline Mae, 247
Crouse, George William, 253
Cullings, Cora Ethel, 246
Dodds, Edward E., 259
" Robert William, 261
" Veda Irene, 260
Ernest, Albert Schuyler, 189
" Alfred Cookman, 98
" George Schuyler, 191
" Gordon, 188
" Harry Liddle, 100
" Helen M., 192
" John Fletcher, 190
" Marion, 187
" Richard Schuyler, 97
" Robert, 193
" William E., 99
Fideler, Charles Myron, 216
" John Ward, 215
" Nathan Hale, 217
Gay, Conklin George, 211D
Hines, Doris A., 257
" Charles Delos, 258

Ingersoll, Alexander, 138
" Edward Liddle, 240
" George Alexander, 239
" John Abbot, 238
" John L., 139
" Nettie, 137
" Sarah Kathern, 140
" Sarah Janette, 241
Jones, Alexander Liddle, 83
" Amanda Tanner, 158
" Beatta, 80
" Delos, 78
" Harry Amos, 164
" Ida Snell, 157
" Mary Ann, 79
" Mary Elizabeth, 81
" Mary L., 159
" Nancy, 82
" Walter, 156
Liddle, Abbie, 166
" Abigail, 43
" Abram S., 48-77B-128B
" Albertus, G., 92
" Alexander, 6-9-18-42-69-197
" Alexander Thomas, 53
" Ann, 19
" Ann Elizabeth, 45
" Anna Mabel, 130-196
" Andrew G., 105
" Angus, McDermit, 50
" Arthur, 119
" Augusta, 124
" Bertha, 176-155C
" Barbary G., 195
" Beverly Raymond, 231C
" Carrie V., 143
" Cathern Maranda, 144
" Chester L., 178
" Christy, 4
" Charles, 46
" Charles Henry, 150-218
" Clara, 155A
" Clarence Romeyn, 131-134
" Cora Belle, 147
" Dewitt, 230

Liddle, Duncan Robinson, 51
" Earl, 175
" Edith, 198
" Edna, 155B
" Eilene Hutchins, 250
" Elizabeth, 5-15-60-73
" Ella Jane, 146
" Ellen Dianthia, 128C
" Ernest William, 128A
" Eveline, 265
" Frances M., 120
" Francis W., 88-120
" Frank, 142
" Fredrick, 221
" George Thomas, 71-148
" Hazel K., 177
" Helen, 136-219-266
" Henry Raymond, 129
" Henry S., 155
" Ida Ann, 74
" Ida Marie, 34
" Inez, 232
" Isabelle, 231
" Jacob, 122
" James, 22-35-93-194
" Jane, 14-24-173
" Janet Ella, 96
" Janette, 7-123
" Jeanette, 31-52-106
" Jennie B., 127
" Jessie Alice, 248
" John, 8-12-20-32-91
" John Augustus, 58
" John E., 52A
" John Milton, 149
" John Sidney, 84
" Kenneth, 252
" Laura, 199
" Leah Jeanette, 56
" Lina May, 135
" Louisa Mayturn, 233A
" Luella, 165
" Mahala, 125
" Margaret Isabelle, 57
" Margaret, 3-90
" Mary, 23-44
" Mary Arabelle, 75
" Mary Belle, 126-145
" Mary Cathern, 70
" Mary Elizabeth, 29-94-251
" Mary Ethel, 151

Liddle, Mary Gifford, 77A
" Mary Helen, 59
" Myrtle Mary, 249
" Nancy, 86
" Nettie, 132
" Peter, 11
" Ralph, 174
" Robert, 1-10-16-104-121
" Robert Blood, 33
" Robert Duncan, 25
" Robert G., 128
" Robert James, 55-87
" Robert W., 49-95
" Roberta, 233
" Romeyn, 13
" Sanford E., 256
" Sarah, 30-52B-62-85
" William, 21-26-133
" William Allen, 54
" William E., 89-234B
" William Henry, 72
" William James, 76
" Warren, 77-220
" Zenia, 167
" Stewart Blood, 28
" Thomas, 2-17-27-47-61
Moore, Irene, 245B
Motte, Margaret Crowell, 200
" Mervin Stuart, 201
" Raymond Russell, 202
McClure, Grace, 141
McDugal, Ralph Wesley, 271
McFarlan, Abbie Ann, 111
" Addie Belle, 116
" Barbary Liddle, 115
" Bessie Gibbard, 113
" Charles Liddle, 108
" Charles Spurgen
(Clemens) 212
" Eva Xelia, 107
" Jennie Lyle, 110
" Kate Vedder, 117
" Margaret Lena, 109
" Martha Ramsey, 118
" Mary Gifford, 114
" Sarah Jane, 112
McMillan, Anna B., 141E
" Andrew Thomas, 63
" Benjamin, 67
" Florence, 141B
" Frank, 141A

McMillan, James, 65
" Jessie B., 141G
" John D., 141F
" John Alexander, 64
" Mary, 141C
" Mary Jane, 245A
" Mary Jane, 68
" Robert, 66
" Samuel, 141D
Quick, Andrew G., 267
Scace, Raymond L., 263
" Robert W., 262
Sears, Florence May, 227
" William Carlton, 226
Seaver, Gertrude, 182
" Leonard William, 184
" Ruth, 183
" Vivian M., 181
Serviss, Alexander Liddle, 101
Sherbourn, John, 102
Spencer, Annabelle, 270C
" Charles Crawford, 211C
" James Wallace, 211B
" Vera Elizabeth, 211A
Spring, Gladys Liddle, 186
" Seymour O., 185
Starr, Clara Barton, 214
" Neal Dow, 213
Terpaning, Alma, 222
" Harold L., 221A

Terpaning, Lucy Lee, 223
" Max, 225
" Mary Jane, 224
Troyes, Bessie I., 228
" Paul D., 229
Van Patten, Arthur, 170
" Dorothy Helen, 254
" Fremont, 172
" Howard, 171
" Ida Belle Liddle, 168
" Ida Virginia, 255
" Irven Roy, 154
" Justus Wright, 153
" Sarah Smith, 169
" William Henry, 152
Vedder, Earl Ingersoll, 236
" Leland Nelson, 235
" Zerah, 237
Wagner, Pauline E., 264
Wilson, Clara Belle, 180
Wood, Bessie Jane, 270B
" Percy Clifford 270A
Wright, Alice Morgan, 103
" Edward, 41
" Henry R., 38
" Jane E., 37
" John, 36
" Robert, 40
" Thomas, 39

INDEX

Adam Liddle Branch

The John, Robert and Adam branches are each numbered separately beginning with "1." The number affixed to a name represents not a page number, but the genealogical number assigned to that person. Care should be exercised in referring to the Adam Liddle branch for names on this page.

Baker, Celestia Lucile, 73
"   Emma Josephine, 71
"   Ethel Marie, 74
"   Joe Flournoy, 72
"   Lillian Mataroe, 70
"   John Lewis, 69
Cooley, David Everett, 68
"   Le Verrier, 67
Everett, Charles A., 33
"   Charles Edward, 65
"   Dona Liddle, 36
"   Elere, 34
"   George William, 35-66
"   Janice, 60
"   Le Ree Welsh, 64
Flournoy, Bertie Rosa, 37
"   Emma, 41
"   Homer Edward, 38
"   Jacob T., 40
"   Lillian, 39
"   Marie, 42
Gillis, David Wiley, 63
"   Mary Elizabeth, 61
"   Norman Everett, 62
Handy, Harvey Downey, 19
"   Minerva, 18
Liddle, Adaline Minerva, 7
"   Adam, 3
"   Adam Perry, 8
"   Anna Alzira, 10
"   Arthur Bloomfield, 28
"   Carl, 47
"   Charles M. Jr., 56
"   Charles McNeil, 12
"   Elizabeth, 48
"   Edward Bloomfield, 31
"   Ella Rosa Bell, 16
"   Frank J., 13
"   Florence, 49

Liddle, Gladys Bloomfield, 32
"   Helen Emma, 15
"   Horace Bloomfield, 30
"   Howard, 51
"   John Grant, 23
"   Jacob T. Jr., 29
"   Jacob Tompkins, 5
"   John Griffith Crapsey, 11
"   John Perry, 4
"   J. T. 3rd, 57
"   Lyla Odette, 55
"   Mary Effie, 14
"   Mildred, 50
"   Moses, Grandson
        Washington, 9
"   Olive May, 46
"   Perry Eugene, 22
"   Ralph, 52
"   Tryphosa Jeanette, 6
"   William Robert Lee, 17
Murrey, Clarence Dale, 54A
"   Dale Stanley, 77
"   Donald Clarence, 78
"   Fern Bolsom, 76
"   Fred Bolsom, 75
Partridge, Allie (Alzira) C., 20
"   Rosella J., 21
Richtmyer, Estella Maria, 24
"   Eva Eliza, 27
"   Rodella A., 25
"   Sarah Addie, 26
Salmen, Elarose Liddle, 43
"   Frederick William, 44
"   Lee Liddle, 45
Tryon, Charles Aubrey, 53
"   Retta Margery, 54
Watkins, Gertrude Armstrong, 59
"   Gladys Liddle, 58